EATS

FOREWORD BY
HESTON
BLUMENTHAL

GQ

EDITED BY
PAUL HENDERSON

THE COOKBOOK
FOR MEN OF
SERIOUSLY
GOOD TASTE

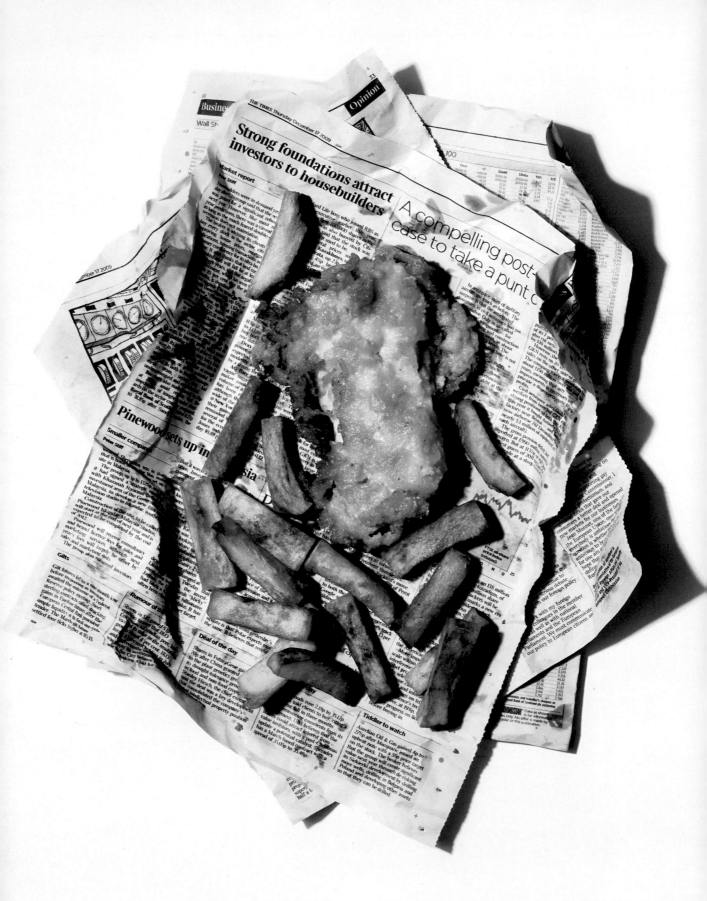

Contents

Foreword
Heston Blumenthal

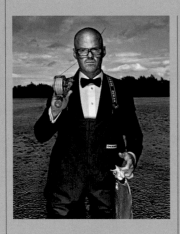

The 1960s in Britain saw an explosion of creativity and we became world-leaders in fashion, music, art and design. The Mini, the Beatles, Carnaby Street – we had it going on. (Or, as Austin Powers put it, *Yeah, baby, yeah!*)

But not in cuisine. Sure, a smattering of trattorias and bistros and espresso bars opened in London at that time. And Michael Caine made omelette-making seem seriously stylish in *The Ipcress File*. But in the main British food somehow missed out on the spirit of the 60s. I've always been a bit disappointed and puzzled by this. Was it a hangover from post-war austerity? (After all, rationing only finished for good in 1954.) Were we still intimidated by the vigour and confidence of French cookery? Whatever the reason, British cuisine was unimpressive and unexciting: a by-word for bad food in many countries around the world.

Until the late 1980s, that is, when things began to change. Keith Floyd's edgy, unpredictable TV shows awakened the nation's appetite for food as a spectator sport. Young, hungry British chefs started grabbing Michelin stars (and newspaper headlines for their antics in and out of the kitchen). Cooking had finally become cool.

GQ has, of course, been a part of this (it, too, first appeared in the late 80s), tracking down the hippest restaurants, profiling up-and-coming chefs, featuring the latest recipes and trends, and presenting it all in striking and dramatic photography.

Over the years I've graced the mag's pages wearing a mackerel as a tie; in the middle of a lake in thigh-high waders and misted-up specs; and in front of a garden shed with a duck on my shoulder. For one shoot they put me in a Brioni suit. At the time I worked all day every day in chef's whites and spent what little downtime I had in tracksuit bottoms and Timberlands, so the sharp lines and beautiful tailoring of that suit were a revelation – James Bond, apparently, liked a bit of Brioni – so I bought the suit and wore it to death. For another shoot, it was suggested I lie in a bath of pig's blood – see what I mean about dramatic? – but that is most definitely where I drew the line!

For me it was an incredible thrill to appear in a magazine because, when I was originally inspired to become a chef at sixteen, it wasn't just the cooking that got me going (though that was a huge part of it), it was the whole idea of being a chef: the glamour of it all, from the heat of the kitchen and the fast pace and pressures of service to the incredible elegance of the restaurants and their food. I used to pore over the photos in books like *Great Chefs of France* that showed my idols cooking up a storm in the kitchen, or checking out shellfish in the local market, or blind-tasting a new vintage of Sancerre down in the *caves*. At that stage – and for a long time afterwards, even after the Fat Duck first opened in 1995 – I never imagined that I'd get to do something similar in the pages of a magazine. I've been GQ's Chef of the Year three times (the first of these, in 2005, was the first red-carpet event I ever attended) and for the last few years I've written a column for the mag on everything from a tally of top Tokyo restaurants to a piece in praise of pork scratchings.

In the last five years or so there has, I think, been a real food revolution in this country. Even in the 90s and noughties, as food became sexy and fun and fashionable in Britain, we were still basically cooking a version of the French classical tradition and had a relatively conservative approach. (Certainly when I first started cooking with liquid nitrogen, for example, or flavour-pairing or developing multi-sensory dishes or creating savoury ice creams – all of which are now standard in many modern high-end restaurants – there was a fair amount of disapproval and resistance, even from other chefs.) There was technical merit aplenty, but not yet a distinctive culinary identity of our own. That, it seems to me, has now changed (which of course makes cooking in this country even more exciting!). Now, there's a clear pride in British dishes and a newfound curiosity about our culinary history. British chefs no longer feel obliged to follow the French model and, as a result, we've found our own voice – committed to British ingredients, playful and ironic, iconoclastic and inventive yet respectful of tradition. It's incredibly exciting to see and be a part of.

If cooking really is the new rock and roll – and why not? – then *GQ* has been helping spread the word with mouthwatering recipes and ineffably cool pics – as you'll see in the pages that follow. Enjoy.

BRILLIANT

BREAKFASTS

Buttermilk Pancakes
Sujan Sarkar | Automat

These perfect pancakes are a breakfast favourite at this New York-style brasserie located in the heart of London's Mayfair. A tempting stack of classic, light and fluffy Americana is the perfect way to start the day when served with a rich and sweet blueberry compote (and don't forget the maple syrup).

MAKES 12

For the blueberry compote
250g (9oz) blueberries
25ml (¾fl oz) water
50g (1¾oz) caster sugar

For the batter
125g (4oz) plain flour
10g (¾oz) baking powder
pinch of salt
15g (½oz) caster sugar
250ml (9fl oz) milk
1 egg
25g (1oz) butter, melted

To serve
maple syrup
icing sugar

1 To make the blueberry compote, place all the ingredients in a pan and simmer slowly until the mixture has a jam-like consistency. Leave to one side.

2 Sift together the flour, baking powder and salt into a large bowl and stir in the sugar.

3 In a separate bowl, lightly whisk together the milk with the egg, then whisk in the melted butter.

4 Pour the milk mixture into the flour mixture, then using a electric hand whisk beat until it forms a smooth batter. Leave to stand for 15 minutes before using.

5 Heat a large nonstick frying pan over medium heat and spray in a little oil. Ladle a spoonful of batter into the pan and cook for 2–3 minutes on each side or until golden brown. Stack on a warmed plate while you cook the remaining pancakes.

6 Serve 3–4 pancakes per person. Drizzle with maple syrup and top with blueberry compote. Dust with icing sugar before serving.

Chef's Tip
Not so much a tip as an instruction – add a few rashers of crispy bacon to finish off this dish in style.

Eggs Benedict
Patrick Clayton-Malone + Dominic Lake | Canteen

Indulgent but irresistible, Eggs Benedict makes a wonderful brunch or a decadent lunch, but works best as a breakfast that helps you ease your way into a leisurely weekend. This version from Canteen is simple and has been a cornerstone of their breakfast menu for years.

SERVES 4

For the hollandaise sauce
250g (9oz) unsalted butter
4 egg yolks
1 tsp tarragon vinegar
salt
juice of ½ lemon
cayenne pepper

50ml (2fl oz) white wine vinegar
8 organic eggs
4 English muffins
8 slices of smoked British ham

1 Melt the butter in a pan over a low heat, then remove the warm, clear oil and set the butter aside.

2 Put the egg yolks, vinegar, salt and a splash of water in a bowl, place this over a pan of simmering water and whisk until the mixture is pale and thick.

3 Remove the bowl from over the pan, whisk in the melted butter, then add the lemon juice and cayenne. Add more salt if needed.

4 Bring a pan of water to the boil, then add the white wine vinegar. Poach the eggs in the pan for 3–4 minutes until soft.

5 Split and toast the muffins. Layer the ham and egg on the muffin halves and top with a dollop of hollandaise sauce.

Chef's Tip
Making a smooth, full-bodied hollandaise sauce can be tricky. Keep the heat very low and use a metal whisk. Vigorous whisking protects the eggs from overcooking and incorporates air into the emulsion.

Breakfast Burrito
Bruno Pires | Tortilla

The traditional breakfast burrito has a bad rep for being a bad wrap but, thanks to some clever substitutions by chef Bruno Pires, this one is heart-warming rather than heart-warning. 'My version removes potatoes and cheese, includes egg whites instead of whole eggs, and uses boiled chicken instead of chorizo,' says Pires, 'so you'll get the flavour without the fat.'

SERVES 4

4 flour (or wholemeal) tortillas
low-fat soured cream

For the black beans
500g (1lb 2oz) pack of
  black beans
½ onion, cut into chunks
2 garlic cloves, roughly chopped
½ **tbsp** salt
½ **tbsp** oregano
½ **tbsp** ground cumin

For the chicken
4 chicken breast fillets
1 onion, quartered
4 garlic cloves, cut into 4 pieces
1 tbsp salt
1 tbsp paprika
juice of **1** lime

For the pico de gallo (salsa)
4 ripe red tomatoes, diced
1 onion, diced
handful of fresh coriander,
  chopped
1 tsp salt
1 tsp olive oil
juice of **1** lime
jalapeño chilli, chopped
  (optional)

For the eggs
4 medium egg whites
2 tbsp skimmed milk
pinch of salt

1 Soak the beans overnight in 2 litres (3½ pints) of cold water.

2 Put the beans in a pan with sufficient water to cover the beans by a few inches. Add the remaining black beans ingredients and bring the water to the boil.

3 Boil the beans for roughly 1 hour until they are soft (you should be able to squash them between your fingers easily). Add more water, if necessary, to keep the beans covered.

4 Meanwhile, bring another pan of water to the boil and add the chicken fillets, onion, garlic, salt and paprika. Poach the chicken for around 30 minutes until tender.

5 Shred the cooked chicken with a fork, then transfer it to a bowl and squeeze over the lime juice. Set aside.

6 Mix together all the ingredients for the pico de gallo in a bowl and set aside.

7 Put the egg whites and milk in a bowl, then beat together and mix in the salt.

8 Heat a nonstick frying pan over a medium-high heat. Add the eggs and scramble to your desired consistency.

9 To serve, heat up a tortilla in a frying pan for around 10 seconds until a few bubbles appear. Remove from the heat and transfer to a plate.

10 Add scoops of eggs, beans, chicken and 1 tablespoon each of soured cream and pico de gallo. Wrap and enjoy. Repeat for the remaining tortillas.

Truffled Egg Toast
Rachel O'Sullivan | Spuntino

'This sinful little dish really caught everyone's imagination when we first opened the restaurant in 2011,' says Rachel O'Sullivan. A killer combination of crunch, carb, egg, cheese and truffle oil makes your eyelids droop and produces a moan from deep in the throat.

SERVES 1

3cm (1¼in) thick slice of square white bread
150g (5½oz) grated fontina cheese
2 free-range egg yolks
1 tsp truffle oil
sea salt flakes and freshly ground black pepper

1 Preheat the oven to 180°C/fan 160°C/350°F/gas mark 4.

2 Lightly toast the slice of bread on both sides. Place the slice on a baking sheet and, with a very sharp knife, cut a shallow well of about 5cm (2in) square into the centre of the bread. (To do this, cut the outline of the well and press down the toasted bread inside the cut lines to create the well.)

3 Distribute the grated fontina evenly around the well. Pour the egg yolks into the well. Place the baking sheet into the oven and toast for about 3 minutes until the cheese melts.

4 Take out the toast, stir the runny yolks, drop the truffle oil in dribbles on to the surface and throw on a little salt and pepper. Eat immediately.

Chef's Tip
The best bread for this is one of those square white farmhouse loaves. Buy it uncut so that you can cut a slice of the size you want.

Parmesan Grits with Wild Boar Sausages and Soy-Pickled Mushrooms

Miles Kirby | Caravan

Grits is a food of native American origin and is similar to other corn-based porridges such as polenta. It can be a bit bland, but with the right flavourings and some bold, gutsy accompaniments, grits is utterly delicious... as in this recipe from Miles Kirby at Caravan.

SERVES 4–6

400ml (14fl oz) milk
50g (1¾oz) butter
50g (1¾oz) cornmeal grits or yellow polenta
40g (1½oz) crème fraîche
75g (2½oz) Parmesan cheese, grated
salt and freshly ground black pepper
4–6 large wild boar (or coarsely ground pork) sausages (1 per serving)
grated Parmesan cheese, to serve

For the soy-pickled mushrooms
50ml (2fl oz) vegetable oil
1 small onion, diced
2 garlic cloves, crushed
400g (14oz) wild mushrooms (mixed varieties)
60ml (2¼fl oz) light soy sauce
60ml (2¼fl oz) water
3 spring onions, finely sliced
4 tbsp chopped flat leaf parsley
white truffle oil
salt and freshly ground black pepper

1 To make the grits, bring the milk and butter to the boil in a medium saucepan. Add the grits or polenta and cook for 3 minutes, stirring constantly.

2 Remove from the heat and allow the grits to cool a little. Stir in the crème fraîche and Parmesan, then season with salt and pepper to taste.

3 Place a lid on the pan and set it aside in a warm place while you prepare the mushrooms. Stir the grits occasionally to prevent a skin or lumps developing. It should have the consistency of thick, creamy porridge.

4 Grill the sausages until cooked through, then slice them into 1cm (½in) rounds. Set them aside until assembly time.

5 In a large frying pan, heat the oil and gently sauté the onion and garlic.

6 Add the mushrooms to the pan and turn up the heat. Sauté the mushrooms for about 3 minutes until brown and soft.

7 Pour the soy sauce and water into the pan and reduce by half. Stir in the spring onions and parsley. Finally, add the truffle oil and season with salt and pepper.

8 To serve, spoon the grits into a 1cm- (½in-) thick 'pool' in the centre of a large plate for sharing. Scatter the pickled mushrooms evenly over the grits, letting the juice from the pickle fill any shallow points. Arrange the sausage slices evenly over the plate, sprinkle over more Parmesan and serve.

Bacon Naan
Naved Nasir | Dishoom

A bacon sarnie, but not as you know it. Naved Nasir from Dishoom offers an Indian twist on the British breakfast staple with the use of naan and tomato-chilli jam. It's difficult to get the bread just right without a tandoor oven, but this version should be pretty good if you decide to make your own.

SERVES 4

For the tomato-chilli jam
200g (7oz) canned tomatoes
20g (¾oz) fresh root ginger, finely chopped
2 garlic cloves, finely chopped
1 small green chilli, finely chopped
30ml (1fl oz) rice vinegar
75g (2½oz) sugar

For the naan breads
190g (7oz) strong white bread flour, plus extra for dusting
pinch of salt
½ **tsp** baking powder
10g (¼oz) natural yogurt
½ **tsp** granulated sugar
20ml (⅔fl oz) milk
⅓ egg, beaten
10ml (⅓fl oz) vegetable oil
75ml (2½fl oz) water

3 rashers of smoked back bacon per person
80g (3oz) Philadelphia cheese
a few sprigs of fresh coriander, leaves picked

1   To make the tomato-chilli jam, process the tomatoes in a blender for 15 seconds to make a purée. Add all the other tomato-chilli jam ingredients except for the sugar and process for another 15 seconds.

2   Put the mixture in a pan and stir in the sugar. Cook over a low heat for approximately 10 minutes or until the mixture has a thick consistency, then allow to cool.

3   Sift the flour, salt and baking powder into a mixing bowl. In another bowl, whisk together the yogurt, sugar, milk and beaten egg.

4   Make a well in the centre of the flour and add the egg mixture. Knead to make a soft dough, then allow to rest for 10 minutes. Add the oil, knead and punch the dough, then cover it with a moist cloth and set aside for 2 hours.

5   Divide the dough into four balls. Place these on a floured surface, cover with clingfilm and allow to rest for 30 minutes. Preheat the oven to 240°C/ fan 220°C/ 475°F/gas mark 9 and heat two oiled baking sheets.

6   Flatten each of the dough balls into a disc and stretch it out into a naan bread shape. Place these on the prepared baking sheets. Bake for 2–3 minutes until crispy, sprinkling occasionally with the water.

7   When ready to serve, grill the bacon. Spread the cheese on half of a naan bread. Place the bacon rashers over the cheese. Drizzle with some of the tomato-chilli jam. Sprinkle over the coriander leaves and fold the naan in half. Serve with more jam on the side, for dipping.

Courgette and Manouri Fritters
Yotam Ottolenghi | Nopi

For an alternative and ever-so-slightly addictive start to the day, these courgette and manouri fritters are quick and easy to prepare and very tasty. If you can't get hold of manouri cheese, don't worry – this recipe works just as well with feta or goats' cheese.

SERVES 4
MAKES 12 FRITTERS

200g (7oz) soured cream
2 tbsp chopped fresh coriander
1½ tsp ground cardamom
2 tsp sunflower oil, plus extra
  for frying
grated zest and juice of **2** limes
salt and freshly ground
  black pepper
3 medium courgettes, grated
2 small shallots, finely chopped
2 garlic cloves, crushed
about **60g (2¼oz)** self-raising flour
2 large free-range eggs
2 tsp ground coriander
150g (5½oz) manouri (or feta)
  cheese
sunflower oil
lime wedges, to serve

1 Mix together the soured cream, chopped coriander, half a teaspoon of ground cardamom, sunflower oil, all the lime juice and the zest of 1 lime. Season with salt and pepper to taste, cover and chill until you serve the fritters.

2 Place the grated courgettes into a large bowl. Sprinkle with half a teaspoon of salt and leave for 10 minutes. Squeeze the courgettes to remove most of the liquid, leaving just a little bit of wetness. Add the shallots, garlic, flour, eggs, ground coriander, remaining ground cardamom and remaining lime zest and a pinch of black pepper. Mix all the ingredients well to form a thick batter, then fold in the manouri.

3 Heat a splash of oil in a large frying pan and add heaped dessertspoonfuls of the batter to the pan, flattening each fritter slightly as it cooks. Cook on each side for approximately 3 minutes until golden and crisp. Remove from the pan and leave to drain on a sheet of kitchen paper to remove any excess oil.

4 Serve three fritters per portion with a generous dollop of the soured cream sauce and lime wedges.

Chef's Tip
As an alternative to soured cream, serve the fritters with a dollop of crème fraîche mixed with the grated rind and juice of a lime.

Coconut and Ricotta Pancakes
Anna Hansen | The Modern Pantry

These light and moreish pancakes provide a brilliant alternative to the usual stodgy morning offerings. And serving them with pomegranate syrup really hits the decadent sweet spot.

SERVES 6

150g (5½oz) self-raising flour
1 tsp salt
25g (1oz) caster sugar
50g (1¾oz) desiccated coconut
70g (2½oz) egg yolks
185ml (6½fl oz) buttermilk
65g (2¼oz) melted butter
375g (13oz) ricotta cheese
140g (5oz) egg whites
butter, for frying
400g (14oz) crème fraîche

For the pomegranate molasses and star anise-roasted rhubarb
2 rhubarb sticks, chopped into chunks
1 tbsp demerara sugar
½ tsp ground star anise
3 tbsp pomegranate molasses

1 Preheat the oven to 180°C/fan 160°C/350°F/gas mark 4.

2 Sift the flour, salt and sugar into a large bowl. Add the coconut and mix well.

3 Whisk together the egg yolks, buttermilk and melted butter. Mix this into the dry ingredients. Carefully fold in the ricotta.

4 Whisk the egg whites to slightly firmer than soft peaks and fold them through the batter in three batches.

5 Heat a little butter in an ovenproof pan. Dollop spoonfuls of the batter into the pan. Put the pan into the oven for 4 minutes, then remove and flip the pancakes. Return to the oven for 4 minutes or until the pancakes are cooked. Set aside somewhere warm.

6 Lower the oven temperature to 140°C/fan 120°C/275°F/gas mark 1. Lay the rhubarb chunks in a roasting pan and sprinkle over the sugar, star anise and pomegranate molasses. Roast for 10 minutes. Remove from the oven and leave to cool.

7 Serve the pancakes with the roasted rhubarb and crème fraîche.

Chef's Tip
The batter can be frozen for up to a month. Defrost it overnight in the refrigerator and fold through another 100g (3½oz) ricotta before you cook the pancakes.

Goose Hash
Rowley Leigh | Le Café Anglais

All goose and duck makes excellent hash, especially the fatty bits, but you can also make this dish using turkey (leg meat is best). Whichever bird you use, don't forget that you can top it off with a fried egg and a slug of tomato ketchup for a hearty breakfast to keep you going for hours.

SERVES 4

400g (14oz) large potatoes, peeled and diced into large, even pieces
3 tbsp goose fat (or turkey or bacon fat or, at worst, sunflower oil)
1 onion, finely chopped
1 carrot, finely chopped
1 celery stick, finely chopped
1 green pepper, finely chopped
1 small red chilli, finely chopped
600g (1lb 5oz) goose meat, coarsely chopped
Worcestershire sauce
Tabasco sauce (optional)
poultry stock or gravy
2 spring onions, finely chopped
sunflower oil
4 eggs, fried or poached (optional)

1 Cover the potatoes with cold, salted water, bring to the boil, then reduce the heat and simmer for 20 minutes until completely cooked. Drain the potatoes and set aside.

2 Warm the goose fat in a saucepan, add the onion, carrot, celery, green pepper and chilli and let the vegetables sweat gently for about 10 minutes until soft.

3 Add the coarsely chopped meat and the potatoes, increase the heat and stir well. Add a few drops of Worcestershire sauce (and Tabasco too, if desired) and a few tablespoons of stock or gravy. Cook until the liquid evaporates and the mixture forms a proper hash.

4 Add the chopped spring onions, mix well and remove from the heat.

5 Just before serving, heat a film of oil in a nonstick pan. Add the meat and potato mixture, spreading it out until it forms a cake with a thickness of roughly 1cm ($^{1}/_{2}$in). Continue to fry until the hash produces a good crisp exterior. Turn over the hash, ideally with a flamboyant tossing of the pan or, alternatively, by sliding it onto a plate and inverting the plate over the pan. Repeat the operation until crisp on the other side. Serve immediately, with a fried or poached egg on top, if desired.

Devilled Veal Kidneys on Toast
Richard Turner | Hawksmoor

The definitive man breakfast, this dish of strong and spicy, firm and fiery veal kidneys may be a throw-back to Victorian times, but that shouldn't stop you kick-starting your day with this 21st century version by Richard Turner.

SERVES 1

250g (9oz) veal kidneys
1 tsp paprika
½ tsp cayenne pepper
5ml (⅛fl oz) Tabasco sauce
5g (⅛oz) Dijon mustard
10ml (⅓fl oz) Worcestershire sauce
20ml (⅔fl oz) tomato ketchup
10ml (⅓fl oz) olive oil
pinch of Maldon salt
pinch of freshly ground black pepper
50ml (2fl oz) Madeira
80ml (2½fl oz) double cream
5g (⅛oz) chopped flat leaf parsley
1 thick slice of sourdough bread, chargrilled

1 Firstly, prepare the veal kidneys by removing the outer membranes, then split the whole kidneys and remove the fatty cores. Cut the meat into bite-sized nuggets. Blanch the meat in boiling water for 1 minute. Strain and pat dry, then set aside in the refrigerator.

2 Mix the paprika, cayenne, Tabasco, mustard, Worcestershire sauce and tomato ketchup in a bowl. When completely mixed, add the kidneys and coat the meat completely in the marinade. Leave in the refrigerator to marinate for at least 1 hour.

3 Heat a nonstick frying pan and add the oil. Make sure the pan is very hot, then add the kidneys and the marinade. Season with salt and pepper. Fry the kidneys for a minute on each side. Add the Madeira and cook for a further 2 minutes. Now add the cream, bring to the boil and cook for another minute. Remove from the heat, check the seasoning and stir in the parsley. Serve on a slice of chargrilled bread.

BEST OF

Two-way Braised Rabbit
Simon Schama

This rabbit dish may take a while to cook, but it is neither laborious nor complicated to prepare and is definitely worth the time. Plus you can serve it either as a meaty, gamey stew or, with just a little coarse blending, as a rich and intense pasta sauce.

SERVES 4

3 tbsp plain flour
salt and freshly ground black pepper
1 tbsp smoked Spanish paprika
1 rabbit, weighing approximately 1kg (2lb 4oz), cut into 6 pieces
100g (3½oz) pancetta (or streaky bacon), cubed
1 large onion, finely sliced
4 garlic cloves, finely chopped
2 medium carrots, finely diced
2 celery sticks, chopped
2 leeks, finely chopped
2 tbsp finely chopped flat leaf parsley
1 red pepper, finely chopped
olive oil
1 cinnamon stick, broken in half
6 allspice berries, crushed
1 tbsp coriander seeds, crushed
4 ripe tomatoes, deseeded and chopped (or 1 x 400g/14oz) can Italian tomatoes)
2 tbsp Cognac
large pinch of saffron threads, soaked in **1–2 tbsp** hot water
2 glasses of dry white wine
1 tbsp tomato purée
250ml (9fl oz) chicken stock

To serve as a pasta sauce
500g (1lb) pappardelle
salt
olive oil
200g (7oz) Parmesan cheese, grated
1 tbsp finely chopped flat leaf parsley, to garnish

1 Season the flour with salt, pepper and smoked paprika, then dust the rabbit pieces in the seasoned flour.

2 In a casserole dish, fry the cubes of pancetta until they render their fat. Add the onion, garlic, carrots, celery, leeks, parsley and red pepper and fry over a medium-low heat until soft. Remove the contents of the casserole with a slotted spoon and set aside.

3 Add a splash of olive oil to the casserole, increase the heat to medium-high, add the cinnamon, allspice and coriander, then brown the coated rabbit pieces until golden. Return the vegetables and pancetta to the casserole, add the tomatoes and fry for 2 minutes, stirring all the time.

4 Add the brandy and flambé – stand back! Reduce the heat to medium, add the saffron and a tablespoon of its water, 1 glass of white wine and the tomato purée and allow the ingredients to simmer gently for about 5 minutes, stirring constantly.

5 Add the stock, bring to the boil, then reduce the heat to low. Half cover the pan and simmer gently for 2 hours or until the rabbit meat is falling off the bone and the liquid has been reduced to a rich, meaty sauce.

To serve as a pasta sauce

1 Take the rabbit pieces from the stew and carefully remove all the bones. Finely shred the meat and set aside.

2 Remove the cinnamon and allspice from the vegetables, then blitz the vegetables briefly in a food processor. Don't overdo it – you want this pasta sauce to be rich and coarse.

3 Return the rabbit and vegetables to the pan, add the remaining glass of white wine, bring to the boil, then reduce the heat and simmer over a very low heat for 5 minutes.

4 Cook the pappardelle in salted, oiled water until al dente. Drain the pasta, reserving 3 tablespoons of the pasta water. Return the pasta to the pot with the pasta water, shake and stir in the rabbit sauce. Serve with freshly grated Parmesan and a sprinkling of parsley.

Dressed Crab with Celeriac
Gary Lee | The Ivy

The Ivy remains the quintessential London restaurant and yet, under the watchful eye of Executive Chef Gary Lee, the menu has continued to evolve. 'We are an institution,' says Lee, 'but we have to be daring, hence new and improved dishes like this dressed crab with celeriac.'

SERVES 1

150g (5½oz) brown crab meat
1 tsp tomato ketchup
1 tsp Worcestershire sauce
2 tsp English mustard
5g (⅛oz) gelatine leaves
juice of ½ lemon
60–70g (2¼–2½oz) brown bread, crusts removed, broken into small pieces
50ml (2fl oz) vegetable oil mixed with **50ml (2fl oz)** olive oil
salt and freshly ground black pepper
110g (3½oz) white crab meat
handful of mustard cress
good-quality brown bread, toasted

For the celeriac rémoulade
1 small head of celeriac, peeled and finely shredded
juice of ½ lemon
2 tsp English mustard
salt and freshly ground black pepper

For the vinaigrette
50ml (2fl oz) olive oil
100ml (3½fl oz) vegetable oil
40ml (1½fl oz) white wine vinegar
70g (2½oz) Dijon mustard
½ tsp caster sugar
salt and freshly ground black pepper

1 Make a brown crab mayonnaise the day before you intend to serve the dish. Mix the brown crab meat, ketchup, Worcestershire sauce and mustard in a blender.

2 Melt the gelatine in the lemon juice and add this to the crab with the bread. Process in the blender. Trickle in the oil as you blend. When the mixture has a smooth texture, place it in a bowl. Season with salt and pepper, cover and refrigerate.

3 About 1 hour before you intend to serve the dish, spoon the white crab meat into a 6cm (2 ½ in) ring mould. Spoon the brown crab mayonnaise on top, then refrigerate for 1 hour.

4 Soak the celeriac in a bowl of cold water with the lemon juice for about 1 hour.

5 Drain the celeriac and dry it on some kitchen paper or in a salad spinner.

6 Mix together all the ingredients for the vinaigrette thoroughly, either in a blender, by whisking them by hand or by pouring them into a clean empty jam jar and shaking.

7 Whisk together the vinaigrette with the mustard. Toss the celeriac in the dressing and season to taste with salt and pepper.

8 Transfer the crab to serving plates and garnish with mustard cress. Serve with toast and celeriac rémoulade.

Lancashire Hotpot
Billy Reid | St Pancras Grand Restaurant

A classic Northern dish, hotpot is the perfect comfort food for winter. Billy Reid's recipe is based on a traditional version his mother used to make, which has been handed down from generation to generation.

SERVES 4

4 carrots, sliced
salt and freshly ground black pepper
4 lamb neck fillets, sinew and cartilage removed, each cut into 5 pieces across the length
2 onions, sliced
2 chicken stock cubes dissolved in **1.2 litres (2 pints)** boiling water
4 large potatoes, peeled and finely sliced
55g (2oz) butter

1 Preheat the oven to 180°C/fan 160°C/350°F/gas mark 3. Season 4 ovenproof earthenware pie dishes, each measuring roughly 13cm (5in) wide, with salt and pepper, then add a layer of the sliced carrots to the bottom of each dish.

2 Season the lamb neck fillet with salt and pepper and place a fillet in each dish on top of the carrot layer. Add a layer of sliced onion, then a second layer of carrot.

3 Divide the hot stock between the pie dishes, then arrange a neat layer of the fine potato slices on top of the dishes, using approximately three potato layers in each dish. Season with salt and pepper and place a knob of butter on top of each dish.

4 Place the dishes into a roasting pan with about 2.5cm (1in) water in the bottom. Cover the roasting pan with silicone paper, then with foil. Cook in the oven for 2 hours. Serve with pickled red cabbage and green beans.

Chef's Tip
The best accompaniment to hotpot has to be pickled red cabbage.

Bubble and Squeak
Mark Hix | Hix

Although bubble and squeak is traditionally made from leftovers, Mark Hix is such a fan of the dish, he happily recommends making it from scratch whenever the urge strikes. This gratifying dish is perfect served at any time of the day. (And, contrary to rumour, bubble and squeak is not best served with a hangover.)

SERVES 4

60–75g (2½–3oz) swede, peeled and cut into rough 1cm (½in) chunks
125–150g (4–5oz) Charlotte (or similar waxy) potatoes, peeled and cut into rough 1cm (½in) chunks
200g (7oz) green cabbage, chopped
1 leek, trimmed and roughly chopped
100g (3½oz) Brussels sprouts, trimmed and halved
1 tbsp chopped fresh parsley
salt and freshly ground black pepper
celery salt
Worcestershire sauce (optional)
plain flour, for dusting
2 tbsp of clarified butter or vegetable oil, for frying

1   Cook the swede and the potatoes in boiling water. When they are cooked, drain, then roughly chop and set aside.

2   Cook the cabbage, leek and Brussels sprouts again in boiling water. When they are just cooked (they should have a slight bite), drain, then chop to the same size as the swede and potatoes. Set aside.

3   Mix all the veg together and stir in the chopped parsley. Season with salt, pepper and celery salt to taste (add a dash of Worcestershire sauce if desired). Mould the mixture into four even-sized flat patties and lightly dust with flour.

4   Heat the butter or oil in a non-stick frying pan and cook a patty for 3–4 minutes on each side or until golden. Keep warm in a low oven while you cook the remaining patties.

Chef's Tip
If you want to make a meal out of bubble and squeak, try serving it with a fried duck's egg and some wild mushrooms fried in butter with a little chopped garlic, or even some devilled lamb's kidneys.

Potted Shrimps on Toast
Simon Wadham | The Rivington Grill

Ideal as a snack or as a starter, potted shrimps have enjoyed something of a culinary renaissance since the dark days of dreary seaside resorts and 1970s dinner parties. Served simply with toast and a thick slice of lemon, you can't go wrong.

SERVES 6

125g (4½oz) unsalted butter at room temperature
juice of ½ lemon
¼ tsp ground mace
¼ tsp cayenne pepper
½ tsp anchovy essence
500g (1lb 2oz) cooked, peeled brown shrimps
salt and freshly ground black pepper
6 slices of wholemeal bread
6 lemon wedges, to serve

1   Put the softened butter into a pan, add the lemon juice, mace, cayenne pepper and anchovy essence and simmer over a low heat for 1 minute to infuse the spices. Remove the pan from the heat and allow the mixture to cool until it is just warm.

2   Add the shrimps, season with salt and pepper and mix well. Refrigerate until firm.

3   About 15 minutes prior to serving, remove the mixture from the refrigerator and allow it to warm to room temperature.

4   Toast the bread, then divide the shrimps mixture over the toast while it is still hot, add a wedge of lemon per serving and serve to your guests immediately. The heat from the toast should allow the butter to melt a little, releasing the flavour.

Fish Pie
Robert Wright | The Gurnard's Head

Having taught at Jamie Oliver's Fifteen and head-cheffed his way around London, Robert Wright is now based in Cornwall, where he was inspired to create this rich and delicious fish pie.

SERVES 4

1kg (2lb 4oz) mashing potatoes, peeled and cut into chunks
salt
125g (4½oz) butter, plus extra for greasing and dotting
freshly ground black pepper
2 tbsp extra fine capers
bunch of curly parsley, all but a few stalks chopped
600g (1lb 5oz) firm white fish fillets, such as ling, pollack or cod
175g (6oz) naturally smoked haddock fillets
750ml (1⅓ pints) whole milk
1 medium onion, roughly chopped
1 large carrot, roughly chopped
1 celery stick, roughly chopped
1 bay leaf
1 tsp peppercorns
75g (2½oz) plain flour
2 tsp Dijon mustard
2 handfuls of cooked, peeled prawns
2 handfuls of cooked mussels, shells discarded
2 hard-boiled eggs, roughly chopped
50g (1¾oz) Gruyère cheese, grated

Chef's Tip
Substitute a cheese called Keltic Gold for the Gruyère. This pungent cider-washed rind cheese, made in Cornwall by Sue Proudfoot (www.whalesboroughcheese .co.uk), adds the perfect finishing touch to this pie.

1   Put the potatoes in a large pan, cover them with water, add one teaspoon of salt and bring to the boil. Reduce the heat to a simmer and cook the potatoes until the tip of a knife goes in easily. Drain the potatoes, return them to the pan and mash them roughly, adding 50g (1¾oz) of the butter, black pepper to taste, the capers and a handful of chopped parsley. Set aside.

2   Put the fish fillets into a medium-sized saucepan. Add the milk, onion, carrot, celery, bay leaf, a few stalks of parsley and the peppercorns. Heat the milk gently over a low heat. When it simmers, switch off the heat and cover the pan – the fish will continue cooking in the pan. Once the fish is cooked through, stand a colander over a bowl and tip in the fish and milk mixture. Preheat the oven to 200°C/fan 180°C/400°F/gas mark 6.

3   To make the sauce, put the remaining butter into a medium-sized pan and melt it over a medium heat. Add the flour and stir well with a wooden spoon to make a roux. Cook for 3 minutes, stirring. Gently whisk in one-third of the hot fishy milk. The roux will thicken quickly. Add another third of the milk, whisking all the time, then the final third, so you end up with a thick sauce. Season with salt, pepper and the Dijon. Reduce the heat to very low and leave the sauce to bubble for 5 minutes while you prepare the fish.

4   Remove and discard the vegetables, herbs and peppercorns from the fish. Peel off and discard any skin from the fish, then gently feel the flesh between your fingers for bones and remove any that you find. Put the boneless fish on a clean plate.

5   Turn off the heat under the sauce and add the fish. Now add the prawns, mussels and chopped eggs, then the remaining chopped parsley and stir. Season to taste.

6   Generously butter a pie dish and pour in the fish mixture. Spoon over the mash and spread it across the surface of the sauce. Dot extra butter over the top and sprinkle on the Gruyère.

7   Bake the pie for about 25 minutes or until the top is starting to brown and the fishy sauce is bubbling up the sides of the mash.

Bergamot-cured Mackerel

Ashley Palmer-Watts | Dinner By Heston Blumenthal

The humble mackerel is often overlooked because it is thought of as cheap and plentiful. But as Ashley Palmer-Watts (the Executive Chef at Dinner By Heston Blumenthal) maintains, it is a wonderfully versatile fish and its flesh is perfect for curing – in this case, with the citrus fruit bergamot. Mackerel is a cheap fish, but the best thing about it is that it is an oily fish, rich in protein, omega-3 fatty acids and vitamin D.

SERVES 4

25g (1oz) granulated sugar
75g (2½oz) salt
20g (¾oz) bergamot rind
10g (¼oz) lime rind
2g (¹⁄₁₆oz) black peppercorns
10g (¼oz) coriander seeds
4 mackerel fillets, pin-boned
olive oil, for frying

For the mayonnaise
35g (1¼oz) egg yolk
20g (¾oz) Dijon mustard
180g (6oz) arachide oil
10g (¼oz) Chardonnay vinegar
2g (¹⁄₁₆oz) salt
40g (1½oz) lemon juice

For the garlic and anchovy sauce
75g (2½oz) garlic cloves, peeled and degermed
1.2 litres (2 pints) semi-skimmed milk for blanching the garlic
200ml (⅓ pint) semi-skimmed milk
10g (¼oz) panko breadcrumbs
50g (1¾oz) anchovy fillets
40g (1½oz) olive oil
15ml (½fl oz) lemon juice

To serve
peas from **8** fresh pea pods, blanched
16 bull's blood leaves
8 endive leaves, blanched for 5 seconds and cut in half
4 pea shoots
25ml (¾fl oz) olive oil
25ml (¾fl oz) bergamot juice

1 Place the sugar, salt, rind, peppercorns and coriander in a food processor and blitz until finely ground. Spread the mixture on a tray and lay on the fish, flesh-side down. Cover with clingfilm and refrigerate for 2 hours. Rinse the fish under cold water to remove the cure and pat dry with kitchen paper.

2 Place a nonstick pan over the lowest heat. Wipe the base with a thin layer of oil. Put in the fillets one at a time, skin-side down and press down to ensure that all of the skin is in contact with the pan. Cook for 10 seconds or just enough to soften the skin. Place the fillets, flesh-side down, on a tray lined with baking paper and refrigerate until cool.

3 To make the mayonnaise, combine the egg yolk and mustard in a bowl. Slowly incorporate the arachide oil, whisking continuously to emulsify the mixture. Add the vinegar, salt and lemon juice, mix well, then refrigerate.

4 To make the garlic and anchovy sauce, cover the garlic with 300ml (½ pint) milk and add a dash of cold water. Bring to a simmer, then drain and rinse the garlic under cold water. Return it to the pan and repeat this process three more times. Then cover the garlic with the 200ml (⅓ pint) milk and bring to a simmer. Allow it to cook until it is very soft and the milk has reduced in volume.

5 Pour the milk into a jug, blitz with a hand blender until smooth, then add the breadcrumbs and anchovy and blitz again, slowly incorporating the olive oil and lemon juice. Pass the mixture through a fine sieve.

6 Weigh the garlic and anchovy mixture, calculate 30 per cent of its total weight and mix that much mayonnaise into it. Refrigerate until required.

7 When ready to serve, cut each fillet into 4–5 pieces. Spread 1 tablespoon of garlic and anchovy sauce on each plate and place the mackerel pieces on top. Garnish with the fresh peas, bull's blood leaves, endive leaves and pea shoots.

8 Whisk together the olive oil and bergamot juice and drizzle a little around each plate just before serving.

Veal Tail and Pea Soup
Fergus Henderson | St John

As you'd expect from the king of nose-to-tail eating, Fergus Henderson recommends that you make your local butcher your best friend. Veal tails are not the easiest cut to get hold of, but definitely worth the effort of acquiring.

SERVES 4

For the brine
400g (14oz) caster sugar
600g (1lb 5oz) sea salt
12 juniper berries
12 cloves
12 black peppercorns
3 bay leaves
4 litres (7 pints) water

For the soup
8 veal tails
3 carrots, roughly chopped
3 leeks, roughly chopped
4 celery sticks, roughly chopped
4 onions, roughly chopped
2 garlic cloves, roughly chopped
2.5kg (5lb 8oz) veal bones, roasted in a hot oven for ½ hour
1 bundle of fresh herbs (parsley, thyme and a little rosemary)
2 egg whites and their very finely chopped shells
450g (1lb) veal flesh, very finely chopped
1 large leek, very finely chopped
salt and freshly ground black pepper
900g (2lb) fresh peas in their pods, podded

For the brine
1 Put all the brine ingredients into a pot and bring to the boil so the sugar and salt dissolve. Allow to cool, then add the veal tails and refrigerate for 1 week. The day before you want to cook, soak the tails in fresh water overnight.

For the soup
1 Put the vegetables into a pot with the veal bones and herbs bundle. Place the tails on top, cover with water and simmer for 3 hours, skimming as you go.

2 Ensure the tails are thoroughly cooked by piercing with a sharp knife, then gently remove them from the pan and set aside.

3 Strain the broth and chill it thoroughly before clarifying. To clarify, in a bowl, whisk the egg whites with a fork, then mix in the very finely chopped veal flesh, eggshells and leek. Whisk this mixture into the cold broth, place it on the heat and bring it to a gentle simmer. Do not stir the broth again. Once the crust is reasonably firm, maintain a gentle heat and lift it off with a slotted spoon. Allow the broth to cool completely.

4 Strain 2 litres (3½ pints) of the broth through a cheesecloth, return to the heat and season with salt and pepper. Reintroduce the tails and heat through. At the last moment, add the peas and serve.

Chef's Tip
Whatever you do, don't scrimp on the brining time. And then don't forget to thoroughly soak the tails in fresh water to desalinate them.

Ham, Egg and Chips
Tristan Welch | Launceston Place

'This recipe turns the most traditional of dishes on its head,' says Tristan Welch. Soaking the gammon removes the salt content and swapping celeriac chips for traditional spuds cuts out a lot of fat. In other words, here's a porky British-food favourite that won't turn you into a pig.

SERVES 4

500g (1lb 2oz) smoked gammon joint
1 large head of celeriac, cut into chips
rapeseed oil, for frying
freshly ground black pepper
1 small bottle of ale
4 fresh eggs

1 The day before you intend to serve this dish, cut the gammon joint into 4 steaks, slicing against the grain of the meat. Now immerse the steaks in cold water and leave them in the refrigerator to soak for 8–12 hours, changing the water at least 4 times to help remove the excess salt.

2 Place the celeriac in a little oil in a hot pan, colour the chips on the stove, then season with pepper. Take them out of the pan and divide them between 4 large sheets of baking paper, placing the chips in the centre of each sheet.

3 Take the gammon out of the water and dry it thoroughly on kitchen paper. Preheat the oven to 180°C/fan 160°C/350°F/gas mark 4.

4 Using the same pan as you used for the celeriac, increase the heat so it's red hot, then sear the steak on one side (there's no need to season the gammon, as it already has a little salt left inside). Then place each steak, seared-side up, on top of the chips.

5 Pour a dash of ale over each steak and chips, then fold the edges of each sheet of baking paper to make a sealed rectangular parcel.

6 Place the parcels on a baking sheet and position this in the centre of the oven. Cook for 12 minutes. Meanwhile, fry the eggs.

7 To serve, tear open the parcels, place a fried egg on top, season with pepper and serve with the rest of the beer (as a treat).

Chef's Tip
Swap the hen egg for a duck egg and a dollop of caviar. You can also add apple cut to the same size as the celeriac and bake it with the ham.

Black Pudding and Treacle Bacon Sandwich
Tom Kerridge | The Hand & Flowers

Is it a burger? Is it a sandwich? Who cares when it tastes as good as this black pudding and bacon bun?! Tom Kerridge's full-flavoured creation is more than a match for any man.

SERVES 4

- **16** rashers of treacle-cured streaky bacon
- **4** ripe plum tomatoes, chopped
- **1** red chilli, chopped
- **1** red onion, chopped
- **100g (3½oz)** brown sugar
- **100ml (3½fl oz)** red wine vinegar
- **1 tbsp** each of coriander seeds, fennel seeds and black peppercorns, plus **2** star anise, all tied together in muslin cloth
- **2** Morris' Gold Medal black pudding rings, thinly sliced
- **2 tbsp** sunflower oil
- **4** brioche buns, split and toasted
- ½ iceberg lettuce, sliced

1 Grill the bacon until it is crispy, then set aside.

2 Put the tomatoes, chilli and red onion in a pan. Add the sugar, vinegar and the muslin bag of herbs and cook for about 20 minutes until you have a thick chutney/paste texture.

3 Fry the black pudding slices in the oil until crispy. Spread some chutney on the base of each toasted bun. Add the black pudding, bacon and more chutney. Finish with lettuce, close the bun and serve.

BOYS'

Veal Chop with Creamed, Sweet and Popped Corn

Jesse Dunford Wood | The Mall Tavern

This meaty and cheeky dish is built around a manly chunky cutlet, but is in touch with its feminine side, thanks to the smooth wet polenta and wilted spinach. Throw in a fun garnish of popcorn and it should appeal to everyone.

SERVES 2

2 veal cutlets, each weighing about 300g (10½oz) each
100g (3½oz) butter, plus extra
1 tsp chopped fresh thyme
salt and freshly ground black pepper
600ml (1 pint) hot chicken stock
2 ears of sweetcorn
250g (8oz) quick-cook polenta
100g (3½oz) popping corn
200g (7oz) baby spinach leaves
lemon wedges, to garnish

1   Smother the veal cutlets in butter, thyme, salt and pepper, then grill for 4 minutes on each side. Leave to rest for 10 minutes in the pan.

2   Heat the butter and stock in a pan, season well, then add the sweetcorn and boil for 5 minutes until tender. Remove the sweetcorn from the stock, carefully shave off the tender kernels and set aside.

3   Whisk the polenta into the boiling stock and cook for 5 minutes until creamy.

4   Either in a pan or in a microwave, pop the popping corn and season well with butter and salt.

5   Warm the sweetcorn kernels with the spinach, wilting them with a little butter in a pan.

6   To serve, place the polenta on plates, put a chop on the polenta base, sprinkle over the spinach and sweetcorn, baste everything with the leftover veal juices and add the warmed popped corn. Garnish with a wedge of lemon.

Lamb and Pistachio Skewers
Silvena Rowe | Quince

For a rugged and earthy taste of Eastern Mediterranean, Silvena Rowe's lamb skewers are given a modern twist with the addition of pistachio and mint. She recommends serving them with a chunky salad and a creamy feta and yogurt dressing.

SERVES 4

400g (14oz) minced lamb
1 onion, grated
3 garlic cloves, crushed
50g (1¾oz) currants
50g (1¾oz) pistachios, roughly chopped
½ tsp sweet paprika
¼ tsp ground allspice
¼ tsp ground cinnamon
½ large bunch of fresh mint, finely chopped
½ large bunch of fresh parsley, finely chopped
salt and freshly ground black pepper
2 tbsp olive oil

1 Combine all the ingredients except the oil in a bowl, season, then form the mixture into kebabs that are about 10cm (4in) long.

2 Put the kebabs onto metal skewers or wooden skewers that have been soaked in water for 30 minutes. Lightly oil the meat skewers using a brush.

3 Grill the kebabs for about 4 minutes on each side. Serve them hot, with a fresh salad and a creamy dressing.

Chef's Tip
Go for the leanest cut of lamb you can before mincing it. You can also use beef or pork to mix things up.

Fried Chicken Nuggets
William Leigh | Wishbone

Setting the trend for delicious, guilt-free fried chicken, food writer and Wishbone chef William Leigh came up with this finger-lickin' recipe for unforgettable nuggets. A word of caution: make then in bulk and have your guests form an orderly queue.

SERVES 2

15g (½oz) togarashi
100g (3½oz) plain flour
pinch of salt
pinch of freshly ground black pepper
2 large eggs
75ml (2½fl oz) milk
200g (7oz) panko or regular breadcrumbs
4 skinless, boneless chicken thighs or breasts, cut into 2.5cm (1in) chunks
1 litre (1¾ pints) vegetable oil, for deep-frying
3 spring onions, sliced
5 shiso leaves or a bunch of mint
2 tbsp toasted sesame seeds togarashi, to garnish

For the sauce
60g (2¼oz) soy sauce
60g rice vinegar or white vinegar
15g (½oz) sugar
1 tbsp togarashi
15ml (½fl oz) liquid from a jar of pickled ginger
2.5cm (1 in) piece of fresh root ginger, finely grated
1 red chilli, finely sliced (optional)

Chef's Tip
Togarashi is a zesty Japanese spice blend and is available in large supermarkets and Asian grocers.

1 First make the sauce: Whisk together all the sauce ingredients in a bowl until the sugar has dissolved. Set aside.

2 Mix the togarashi with the flour, salt and pepper in a bowl. Crack the eggs into a second bowl, add the milk and whisk until smooth. Place the panko crumbs in a third bowl.

3 Dip a piece of chicken into the seasoned flour, tap off the excess, then dip it into the egg. Finally, drop it into the panko crumbs until coated, then set aside on greaseproof paper. Repeat with the remaining chicken pieces.

4 Heat the oil in a high-sided pan until it reaches 180°C/350°F. Fry the chicken pieces in batches until they are cooked through, then drain on kitchen paper.

5 Add the spring onions, shiso or mint leaves and sesame seeds to the sauce. Add the chicken to the sauce, turning each piece over to coat it thoroughly. Arrange the chicken pieces in a serving dish and garnish with more togarashi before serving.

Seekh Kebab
Karam Sethi | Trishna

Although better known for his modern interpretations of cuisine from the southwest coast of India, Karam Sethi created this simple and, more importantly, sustainable fish skewer as the perfect dish for an English summer barbecue.

SERVES 2

For the dill chutney
10 tbsp finely chopped fresh dill
1 tsp finely chopped ginger
1 tsp finely chopped garlic
1 tsp diced shallot
2 tbsp lemon juice
pinch of salt

For the marinade
2 tbsp mustard oil
1 tbsp mustard seeds
25g (1oz) curry leaves
2 tbsp garlic paste
1 green chilli, finely diced
1 tbsp chopped fresh dill
1 tsp English mustard
1 tbsp finely chopped fresh
   coriander
1 tsp salt
2 tbsp lemon juice

For the kebabs
8 roeless scallops
8 large prawns with shells off
   and tail on, deveined
200g (7oz) pin-boned coley,
   cut into 8 chunks

Chef's Tip
You can use any firm white fish for this recipe – monkfish is a good alternative – but coley is recommended for its flavour, texture and natural abundance.

For the dill chutney
1   Place all the chutney ingredients in a food processor and blend to a fine paste.

For the kebabs
1   Make the marinade: Heat the mustard oil in a pan until it reaches smoking point, then add the mustard seeds and curry leaves until they crackle. Remove the pan from the heat and allow the contents to cool, then transfer to a large bowl.

2   Add the remaining marinade ingredients to the mustard oil mixture and stir.

3   Toss the seafood in the marinade until it is well coated, then cover the bowl and leave it in the refrigerator for 30 minutes to marinate. Meanwhile, soak 4 bamboo skewers in hot water for 30 minutes .

4   On to each skewer, thread two pieces of the marinated coley, two scallops and two prawns. Cook the skewers over live coals for approximately 4 minutes on each side.

5   To serve, simply place the cooked skewers on a plate alongside a pot of the dill chutney for dipping.

The Meat Bomb
Charlie McVeigh | The Draft House

What man could resist a Meat Bomb? These hand grenade-sized balls of beef guarantee an explosion of flavour in your mouth and the utter destruction of even the most ravenous hunger.

SERVES 3

For the garlic mayonnaise
2 egg yolks
2 tsp hot Dijon mustard
4 garlic cloves, roasted
2 tsp white wine vinegar
pinch of caster sugar
salt and freshly ground black pepper
50ml (2fl oz) extra virgin olive oil

For the meat filling
100g (3½oz) beef mince
4 shallots, chopped
2 garlic cloves, chopped
200ml (⅓ pint) red wine
400g (14oz) chopped tomatoes
pinch of dried oregano
¼ tsp hot smoked paprika

For the meat bombs
40g (1½oz) butter
50g (1¾oz) plain flour, plus extra for coating
120ml (4fl oz) milk
2 drops Worcestershire sauce
2 drops Tabasco
½ tsp Dijon mustard
40g (1½oz) grated Cheddar cheese
1 egg, beaten
1 packet panko breadcrumbs
300ml (½ pint) vegetable oil, for frying

To serve
20g (¾oz) grated Parmesan cheese
chopped flat leaf parsley

For the garlic mayonnaise
1   To make the garlic mayonnaise, mix the egg yolks, mustard, garlic, vinegar, sugar, salt and pepper in a bowl. Slowly incorporate the oil, whisking continuously to emulsify the mixture. Refrigerate the mayonnaise until you are ready to serve.

For the meat bombs
1   Fry the minced beef until brown, then set it aside. Fry the shallots and garlic in the same pan until they are light brown. Return the meat to the pan, then add the wine and continue to cook until the liquid has reduced by half.

2   Add the remaining ingredients for the meat filling and reduce it all to a thick, dry mixture. Set the filling aside.

3   Melt the butter in a pan, then add the flour and stir until it is cooked. Slowly add the milk over a low heat, stirring constantly, until the mixture has a mashed-potato consistency. Add the Worcestershire sauce, Tabasco, mustard and grated Cheddar and stir until the cheese melts. Take the pan off the heat and leave the mixture to cool.

4   Divide the cheese mixture into 20g (¾oz) pieces and roll each of these into a mini-ball. Press each into a cup shape with your fingers and fill with 10g (¼oz) of the meat filling. Gather the edges of the cheese mixture to seal the meat filling inside. Place the balls on a plate and refrigerate for 1 hour.

5   Dip the balls into plain flour, then in the beaten egg, then roll them in the breadcrumbs. Ensure they are well coated in crumbs.

6   Heat the vegetable oil to 170°C (340°F), then fry the balls until golden.

7   To serve, sit the bombs on top of a dollop of the garlic mayonnaise and sprinkle with Parmesan and chopped parsley.

Chicken Curry (and Rice)
Mark Devonshire | Eckington Manor Cookery School

Johnny Heaf, *GQ*'s Features Director, spent an afternoon in the kitchen and out of his comfort zone learning how to make this sensational chicken curry for the magazine. And if he can do it, anyone can…

SERVES 4

For the chicken curry
1 tsp black peppercorns
1 tbsp coriander seeds
1 tsp cumin seeds
1 tsp fenugreek seeds
1 tsp ground turmeric
4 tbsp vegetable oil
1 onion, thinly sliced
thumb-sized piece of fresh root ginger, peeled and finely chopped
4 garlic cloves, cut into slivers
2 tsp white poppy seeds or ground almonds
400ml (14fl oz) coconut milk
1 tbsp tamarind
5 mild red chillies, deseeded and cut into thin strips
1 tsp salt
4 chicken breasts, sliced into 1cm (½in) pieces
1 sprig of fresh coriander, leaves picked

For *GQ*'s faultless oven-cooked rice
sunflower oil
3 garlic cloves, finely chopped
3 green cardamom seeds
5cm (2in) cinnamon stick
1 bay leaf
350g (12oz) basmati rice
½ tsp salt
600ml (1 pint) water
4 large shallots, finely sliced

1 Preheat the oven to 180°C/fan 160°C/350°F/gas mark 4. Place the peppercorns, coriander, cumin, fenugreek seeds and turmeric in a mortar and use a pestle to grind the whole spices to a fine powder. Set aside.

2 Heat the oil in a large ovenproof pan set over a medium heat, then add the sliced onions, ginger and garlic and cook until they are soft. Next, throw in the ground spices and fry for 2–3 minutes.

3 Add the poppy seeds or ground almonds and the coconut milk, tamarind, three-quarters of the sliced red chillies and ½ teaspoon salt. Bring to the boil, then reduce the heat and add the chicken pieces. Simmer for 5 minutes.

4 Now transfer the pan to the oven and cook for 25 minutes.

5 Remove the curry from the oven, stir in the remaining chillies, check the seasoning (adding the remaining salt if necessary), scatter over the coriander and serve with rice (*see* below).

For GQ's faultless oven-cooked rice
1 Preheat the oven to 150°C/fan 130°C/300°F/gas mark 2. Heat 2 tablespoons of oil in a large ovenproof pan, add the garlic, cardamom, cinnamon and bay leaf and cook for a few seconds until you start to smell the aroma of the spices. Stir in the rice and the salt, add the water and bring to the boil.

2 Transfer the pan to the oven and cook the rice for 10 minutes or until all the water has been absorbed.

3 Meanwhile, fry the sliced shallots in oil with a little salt until golden and crispy, then drain on kitchen paper. Combine the fried onions with the rice to serve.

Meatball Sliders
Andrew Carmellini | Locanda Verde

'This dish is Middle Eastern meets Little Italy in inspiration,'
says Andrew Carmellini of his sensational sliders. 'The surprise
is the goats' cheese centre that oozes out when you bite into them.'
Serve the sliders in a bread roll with pickled cucumber and a layer
of good goats' cheese, preferably Caprino.

SERVES 8–10
MAKES 30 MEATBALLS

3 tbsp extra virgin olive oil
1 small onion, chopped
1 garlic clove, finely chopped
½ tsp ground coriander seeds
1 tsp ground fennel seeds
1 tbsp finely chopped rosemary
225g (8oz) Merguez sausagemeat
450g (1lb) lamb mince
100g (3½oz) dried breadcrumbs
2 eggs
½ tsp salt
25g (1oz) goats' cheese

For the sauce
75ml (2½fl oz) olive oil
1 medium onion, diced
400g (14oz) can San Marzano
  tomatoes and their juices
¼ tsp red chilli flakes
½ tsp salt
½ tsp sugar
½ tsp Sicilian oregano

Chef's Tip
Depending on how tightly
you make your meatballs,
some goats' cheese may
leak out when you cook
them in the sauce. Don't
worry – they will still
taste good.

1   Heat the olive oil in a pan set over a medium heat. Add the onion and sweat for 3 minutes. Add the garlic and cook for 1 minute, stirring constantly.

2   Add the coriander, fennel seeds and rosemary to the pan and cook for 1 minute, so that the aromas of the spices and herbs are released. Transfer the contents of the pan to a bowl and cool in the refrigerator.

3   In a large bowl, combine the sausagemeat and the lamb with the cooled onion-herb mixture, breadcrumbs, eggs and salt. Mix well with your hands.

4   Roll the goats' cheese into 1cm (½in) balls, each roughly the size of a small marble. Place these on a plate and set aside.

5   Divide the lamb mixture into 30 pieces. Take one piece and roll and press it into an oval shape. Use your thumb to create a goats' cheese-ball-sized dent in the middle and drop a goats' cheese ball inside. Pinch the mixture around the ball to seal the opening and roll the meatball between your hands until it is golf ball-sized. Repeat until you've used up all the lamb mixture and goats' cheese balls. Set aside while you make the sauce.

6   Heat the olive oil in a large pan set over a medium-high heat. Add the onion and cook until it starts to soften.

7   Crush the tomatoes with your hand. Add them with their juices to the pan along with the chilli flakes, salt and sugar. Mix well to combine and cook over a medium-high heat for 10 minutes until the flavours combine and the sauce is reduced. Add the oregano and mix well.

8   Add the meatballs to the sauce carefully. Reduce the heat to low, cover and simmer very gently for 10 minutes, turning the meatballs with a small spoon after 5 minutes, until the meat is cooked and the sauce takes on the flavour of the meatballs. It's very important that the liquid never comes to the boil: you want as slow a simmer as possible, so the flavours really come together, the cheese melts and the meat becomes rich and tender.

9   To finish, serve with pickled cucumber in a bread roll with Caprino cheese (or good goats' cheese).

José Dog
James Knappett | Bubbledogs

First came the gourmet burger, now it is all about the hedonists hot dog. Of the wonderfully quirky wieners created by Bubbledogs chef James Knappett, *GQ* recommends the José, in which Mexican meets Americana to fantastic effect.

MAKES 4 DOGS

For the salsa
3 tomatoes, deseeded and diced
juice of **1** lime
1 red chilli, finely chopped
½ red onion, finely chopped
small bunch of fresh coriander, finely chopped
salt

For the avocado sauce
2 avocados
juice of **1** lime
salt

For the hot dogs
4 soft white hot dog buns
4 cooked hot dog sausages
12 jalapeño chillies
soured cream, to serve

For the salsa
Mix all the salsa ingredients together and set aside.

For the avocado sauce
Blitz the flesh from 1½ avocados in a food processor with the lime juice and salt until smooth. Dice the remaining avocado flesh and mix it into the smooth avocado.

For the hot dogs
Cut the buns as if to split them, but keep one side intact so the hot dogs hold together. Spread the insides with the avocado sauce. Add 1 sausage to each bun and top with the salsa. Add 3 jalapeños to each bun and top each hot dog with soured cream.

Chef's Tip
For a truly authentic Bubbledogs experience, why not serve your dogs with a glass of ice cold champagne?

Coq au Vin
Daniel Boulud | Bar Boulud

When Michelin-starred superchef Daniel Boulud opened his first restaurant in London, he based his menu on seasonal French food classics. That's why *GQ* took the opportunity to feature Boulud's definitive version of Coq au Vin, and you won't be disappointed.

SERVES 8

8 chicken legs, thighs and drumsticks separated
1 onion, sliced
1 carrot, sliced
2 celery sticks, sliced
2 heads of garlic, sliced in half
1 herb sachet, made with 8 sprigs of fresh thyme, 1 bay leaf, 2 tsp coriander seeds and 1 tsp cracked white pepper, tied up in a square of muslin with butcher's twine
225g (8oz) slab of bacon, cut into 5mm (¼in) slices
450g (1lb) pearl onions
900g (2lb) small button mushrooms, trimmed
1 x 75cl bottle dry red wine
½ bottle (375ml/12¾fl oz) ruby port wine
salt and freshly ground black pepper
4 tbsp olive oil
4 tbsp plain flour
500ml (18fl oz) unsalted veal stock
500ml (18fl oz) unsalted chicken stock or canned chicken broth

Chef's Tip
Bundling the bacon, pearl onions and mushrooms in muslin means you don't have to fish through the liquid in order to set them aside before straining the sauce.

1 The day before you intend to serve this dish, place the chicken in a large container with the onion, carrot, celery, garlic and herb sachet. Cook the bacon in a large sauté pan set over a medium-high heat until just crispy. Wrap the bacon, pearl onions and mushrooms in separate muslin squares, tie each with kitchen string and add the bundles to the container with the chicken and vegetables. Cover all the ingredients with the red wine and port and marinate in the refrigerator overnight.

2 Next day, preheat the oven to 160°C/fan 140°C/325°F/gas mark 3. Drain the wine from all the ingredients, setting them aside. In a large pot, reduce the wine by half. Meanwhile, pat the chicken dry and season it well with salt and pepper. Heat the olive oil over a medium-high heat in a large casserole dish. Sear the chicken on all sides in one layer. Remove the chicken, add the sliced vegetables and cook, stirring occasionally, over a medium heat for about 6 minutes until soft. Add the flour and cook, stirring, for another 4 minutes.

3 Add the reduced wine, chicken and the mushroom, pearl onion and bacon bundles to the casserole with the veal and chicken stock. Bring to a simmer, cover with a round of baking paper and transfer to the oven. Cook for 1–1½ hours until the chicken is tender.

4 Strain the chicken and vegetables from the sauce and discard the sliced carrot, onion and celery. Remove the bacon, pearl onions and mushrooms from their bundles. If the sauce seems too thin, return it to the heat and reduce until you have the desired consistency (it should coat the back of a spoon). Add the ingredients to the sauce and serve immediately, with fresh pasta or rice. This dish can be kept chilled for up to 4 days.

Veal Cutlet Milanese with Braised Endive
Nic Watt | Aurelia

'This is a big juicy cutlet, but not flattened,' says Nic Watt of his crunchy Italian chop. Full and juicy, it is coated in lemon thyme and Japanese breadcrumbs, then roasted until crispy. And the best accompaniment? That would be a delicious braised winter endive.

SERVES 2

2 veal cutlets
125g (4oz) panko breadcrumbs
2 tsp finely chopped rosemary
4 tbsp finely grated Parmesan cheese
salt and freshly ground black pepper
60g (2½oz) plain flour
2 eggs, whisked
600ml (1 pint) vegetable stock
2 tbsp caster sugar
pared rind from **2** oranges
2 star anise
2 Belgian endive, halved lengthways
2 tbsp butter
2 tsp caster sugar
olive oil, for frying

To garnish
handful of capers
thyme sprigs
sage leaves
flat leaf parsley

1 Gently press the veals into nice full cutlets. Combine the breadcrumbs, rosemary, Parmesan and seasoning in a large bowl and put the flour in another one. Dust the cutlets in plain flour, run through the egg wash, then press them into the seasoned breadcrumbs. Set aside.

2 Combine the vegetable stock, caster sugar, orange rind and star anise in a pan. Add the endives to the stock and gently poach until tender. Take the pan off the heat and drain off the stock. Preheat the oven to 180°C/fan 160°C/350°F/gas mark 4.

3 In a hot frying pan, gently brown the butter and add the endives flat-side down, adding the caster sugar to caramelize them. Cook for about 10 minutes, turning occasionally.

4 In an ovenproof pan, cook the veal cutlets in olive oil for about 2 minutes on either side. Transfer the pan to the oven and cook for a further 6–8 minutes. Serve the veal with the braised endives and garnish with capers, sprigs of thyme, sage leaves and flat leaf parsley.

HEALTH-CONSCIOUS

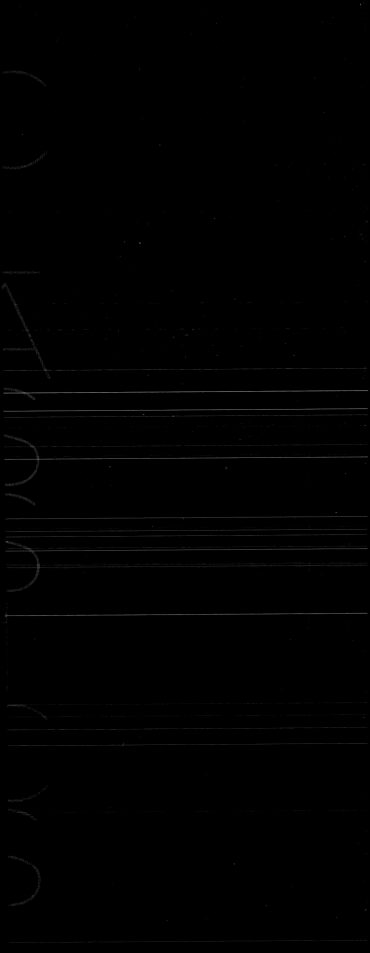

Beef Carpaccio
Heston Blumenthal | The Hinds Head

This easy, quick and delicious carpaccio recipe is brilliant as part of a late-summer salad. The key, however, is getting the very best joint of beef you can find and making sure it is seared in an extremely hot pan.

SERVES 4

For the dressing
50g (1¾oz) finely diced shallots
35g (1¼oz) chopped gherkins
35g (1¼oz) capers
2 tsp Dijon mustard
½ tsp Worcestershire sauce
2 tbsp chopped flat leaf parsley
100ml (3½fl oz) olive oil
2 tsp lemon juice
5 drops Tabasco

For the carpaccio
olive oil
salt, rock salt and freshly ground
  black pepper
500g (1lb 2oz) rolled rump beef
chopped chives, to garnish
freshly grated horseradish,
  to garnish

For the dressing
Put all the dressing ingredients in a food processor and blitz until a coarse paste is formed. Set aside.

For the carpaccio
1   Heat a frying pan over a very high heat until it is extremely hot. Add 2mm (¹/₁₆in) olive oil and continue to heat it until it is smoking hot. Sprinkle a little salt on the rump and sear the meat in the pan for a couple of seconds on each side. Remove the meat from the heat and allow it to cool completely.

2   Once cool, slice the beef as thinly as possible using a very sharp knife. Lay out the slices on 4 plates. Spread a generous layer of the dressing over the top, then sprinkle with rock salt, freshly ground black pepper, chopped chives and freshly grated horseradish.

Chef's Tip
When cutting the beef, it is essential to use a really sharp knife. Allow the meat to cool completely before slicing it as thinly as possible.

Seared Salmon with Avocado, Sweetcorn and Tomato Salsa

David Campbell | The Royal Crescent Hotel

This fresh and light dish of salmon with salsa by David Campbell provides the perfect taste of a British summertime. It also looks quite like an English garden on a plate.

SERVES 4

2 smooth-skinned or Hass avocados, roughly diced
2 plum tomatoes, deseeded and diced into 5mm (¼in) pieces
¼ red onion, chopped
¼ bunch fresh coriander, chopped
rock salt and freshly ground black pepper
1 tsp olive oil, plus extra for dressing the rocket
juice of **1** lemon, plus extra for dressing the rocket
1 x 150g (5oz) can sweetcorn, drained
4 skinless salmon fillets, about 175g (6oz) each
50g (1¾oz) rocket leaves

1. Place the avocados, tomatoes, red onion and coriander in a mixing bowl. Season with rock salt, then add the olive oil and lemon juice. Using a fork, roughly crush the ingredients until they are mixed. Avoid overworking the mixture or it will become soft and mushy.

2. Dry-fry the sweecorn in a hot pan until it starts to char slightly. Add this to the avocado and tomato mixture.

3. Season the salmon fillets on both sides with salt and pepper, then place them in a nonstick heavy-based frying pan and cook for 2 minutes on each side until golden brown on the outside and slightly pink in the middle.

4. To serve, place a neat pile of the salsa in the centre of 4 shallow bowls. Place 1 piece of salmon on top of each pile and garnish with some rocket leaves lightly dressed with olive oil and lemon juice.

Chef's Tip
Use Loch Duart salmon (www.lochduart.com). It is the finest farmed salmon you can get and has the best flavour.

Shepherd's Pie
Stuart Gillies | The Boxwood Café

An indulgent comfort food classic is given a makeover in this dish. Based on an old French housewife's recipe, this version of Shepherd's pie uses roast chicken (you can use leftovers) instead of lamb, and has a carrot and potato topping, which reduces the fat and calorie content without cutting down on flavour.

SERVES 4

1kg (2lb 4oz) Desiree potatoes, peeled and roughly chopped
6 carrots, cut into large dice
salt and freshly ground black pepper
100g (3½oz) crème fraîche
100ml (3½fl oz) semi-skimmed milk
knob of butter
1 cooked medum-sized whole roast chicken, meat removed from the bone
100g (3½oz) Gruyère cheese, grated

1 Place the potatoes and carrots in a pan and cover with cold water. Add a little salt and bring to the boil. Reduce the heat and simmer until the vegetables are tender. Preheat the oven to 190°C/fan 170°C/375°F/gas mark 5.

2 Drain the carrots and potatoes and push them through a potato ricer into a bowl. (If you don't have a ricer, simple mashing will do.) Add to this mixture the crème fraîche, milk and butter and season with salt and pepper. Cover the bowl with clingfilm and keep the contents hot.

3 Take the cold roast chicken meat and place it in a food blender. Blend until the meat is finely chopped, then transfer it to a suitable pie dish. Half-fill this with the chicken meat, then top with the carrot and potato mash. Sprinkle over the Gruyère and bake for about 30 minutes or until golden. Serve the pie immediately.

Chef's Tip
If you want to make this with fresh chicken breasts, be sure to caramelize the meat by frying it in olive oil. Set it aside until cool, then follow the recipe.

The No-bun Burger
Nick Cuadrado

Nick Cuadrado's bunless burger uses Portobello mushrooms instead of bread, extra lean beef and a super tasty relish to great effect – with a fraction of the fat found in a normal burger.

SERVES 2

For the relish
2 shallots, finely diced
2 large gherkins, finely diced
4 tomatoes, skinned, deseeded
   and finely diced
20g (¾oz) chives, finely chopped
1 small chilli, finely chopped

**For the chunky tomato and
mustard ketchup**
3 tbsp wholegrain mustard
juice of ½ lime
1 tomato, diced
1 tsp honey

For the burgers
350g (12oz) finely minced
   feather or onglet steak
salt and freshly ground black
   pepper
olive oil, for frying
4 Portobello mushrooms,
   trimmed
Little Gem heart leaves
beef tomato, sliced
red onion, sliced
1 large gherkin, halved lengthways

For the relish
Mix together all the relish ingredients and set aside.

For the chunky tomato and mustard ketchup
Mix together all the ketchup ingredients and set aside.

For the burgers
1 Season the mince with salt and pepper and knead it into 2 patties 5–7cm (2–3in) in diameter. (A common mistake is to bind the mince with egg and breadcrumbs – doing this can seriously up your calorie intake.)

2 Brush the base of a frying pan with olive oil and pan-fry each patty until pink in the middle, or until well done if you prefer. (Alternatively, grill them if you wish to avoid using the oil.)

3 Place the mushrooms in a roasting pan, season with salt and pepper, then roast in the oven at 200ºC/fan 180ºC/400ºF/gas mark 6 for about 5 minutes or until they are cooked through, but still remaining juicy and succulent.

4 Place two upturned mushrooms on each plate, then place a burger on top of one of them. Pile the onion and tomato garnishes on top of the burgers, with the lettuce leaves on top. Spoon the relish over the lettuce leaves, add a dollop of the tomato and mustard ketchup, then top each pile with the second mushroom and half a gherkin.

Chicken and Chips
Jocelyn Herland + Alain Ducasse | The Dorchester

This nutritious twist on the classic *poulet frites* is fun and fruity, but the real genius is in swapping chips for *panisses fries*, which are made with gram flour. Don't worry – they taste far better than they sound.

SERVES 4

For the chicken
5 oranges
4 chicken breasts
1 lime
1 pink grapefruit
100ml (3½fl oz) olive oil
salt and freshly ground black pepper
1 bunch of spring onions, halved
½ bunch of fresh coriander

For the crispy panisses fries
1 litre (1¾ pints) water
25g (1oz) butter
olive oil
250g (9oz) chickpea (gram) flour
salt and freshly ground black pepper

Chef's Tip
Make the paste for the fries the day before and refrigerate it overnight. Cut it into chips and cook them at the very last minute. When cooking, move them about in the pan so they don't stick.

For the chicken
1 Squeeze the juice of three of the oranges into a bowl and marinate the chicken breasts in the juice for 24 hours.

2 Next day, remove the rinds of the remaining oranges, the lime and half the grapefruit and cut the rinds into strips. Reserve the flesh. Place the rinds in 600ml (1 pint) water, bring to the boil, then reduce the heat and simmer for 5 minutes. Change the water and boil the rinds again, then set them aside.

3 Cut the reserved citrus flesh into 2cm (³⁄₄in) cubes.

4 Remove the chicken from the marinade, reserving the marinade. Heat the olive oil in a casserole dish. Season the chicken breasts and roast them in the casserole, skin-side down, for 2 minutes. Turn the chicken breasts, add the spring onions and cook for 2 minutes, then add the reserved citrus flesh and rinds. Cover the casserole and cook for 3 minutes, then add the marinade and half the coriander. Cook for 10 minutes.

5 Remove the chicken breasts from the casserole and reduce the sauce. Put the chicken breasts back into the casserole with the remaining coriander and heat through. Serve immediately with panisses fries (*see* below).

For the crispy panisses fries
1 Heat half the water with the butter and a dash of olive oil in a large pan. Put the chickpea flour into a bowl and add the remaining water gradually while whipping until the mixture has an even texture. Sieve the mixture well, then pour it into the boiling mix of water, butter and oil and cook over a low heat for 20 minutes while whipping constantly.

2 Pour the paste into an oiled square cake mould, then chase the air from the mould by hitting it. Cover the mould with clingfilm and wait until the paste cools completely, then refrigerate for 6 hours.

3 Remove the paste from the mould and cut it into chip-sized sticks.

4 Heat a frying pan with 2–3 tablespoons of olive oil and cook the fries until they are crispy and golden on both sides. Drain on kitchen paper. Finish by seasoning with salt and pepper.

Chicken Korma
Atul Kochar | Benares

This is a lighter version of the traditionally high-calorie chicken korma, by legendary Indian chef Atul Kochar. With no butter, and using low-fat yogurt and plenty of punchy spices, you'll be hard pressed to tell the difference between this and the full-fat version.

SERVES 1

1½ tbsp vegetable oil
2 garlic cloves, sliced
10 curry leaves
¼ tsp ground black pepper
1 bay leaf
2 cinnamon sticks
2 cloves
3 green cardamom pods
1 star anise
5 medium onions, sliced
1 green chilli, slit lengthways
½ tsp ground turmeric
1 tsp ground cumin seeds
1 tsp ground fennel seeds
4 small Jersey potatoes, washed and halved
400ml (14fl oz) light coconut milk
300ml (½ pint) water
500g (1lb 2oz) chicken breasts, diced, excess fat removed
100g (3½oz) light organic natural yogurt
10cm (4in) fresh root ginger, cut into julienne
2 tsp lemon juice
2 tsp salt

1 Heat the oil in a pan and sauté the garlic without colouring it. Add the curry leaves and other whole spices and fry for 1 minute or until the spices start to crackle, then add the sliced onions and green chilli.

2 Sauté the onion without colouring it for about 5 minutes, then add the turmeric, ground cumin seeds and fennel seeds. Stir, then add the potatoes.

3 Add half the coconut milk and the water and cook the potatoes until they are nearly done.

4 Add the diced chicken and simmer over a low heat for about 20 minutes or until the chicken is just cooked.

5 Whisk the remaining coconut milk with the yogurt, add it to the pan and simmer gently for a few more minutes. Add the ginger for the final few minutes of cooking, and add lemon juice and salt to taste. Serve the curry hot with steamed brown basmati rice (not naan bread and lager).

Fish and Chips
Simon Foster | Milroy's

Fish, chips, mushy peas... only they are good for you. What's not to like? And there's more. 'Not only is this healthy and full of flavour,' its creator, the late Simon Foster, told *GQ*, 'but it also uses pollock, which is a sustainable fish. So you are being kind to the planet as well as yourself.'

SERVES 2

For the fish
80g (3oz) white bread
2 shallots, finely chopped
1 tbsp olive oil, plus extra for greasing
1 large handful of flat leaf parsley, finely chopped
2 pollock or coley fillets, about 400g (14oz) each, skin left on
salt and freshly ground black pepper

For the chips
12 new potatoes, washed
salt and freshly ground black pepper
2 tbsp olive oil

For the pea and mint purée
200g (7oz) peas
olive oil
small handful of fresh mint, chopped
salt and freshly ground black pepper
sprigs of flat leaf parsley, to serve

For the fish
1 Preheat the oven to 220°C/fan 200°C/425°F/gas mark 7. Put the bread in a food processor and blend it to fine breadcrumbs.

2 Sweat the shallots in the olive oil until they are translucent but not coloured. Add the breadcrumbs and chopped parsley, mix to form a moist paste and set aside.

3 Season the fish with salt and pepper. Grease a baking sheet with a little olive oil and place the fish, skin-side down, on the sheet. Spoon the breadcrumb and parsley mixture on top of the fish and gently pat the mixture down to cover the surface of the fish. Bake for 6–8 minutes until the crust is golden brown.

For the chips
1 Cook the new potatoes in boiling salted water for 5 minutes. Drain, cut them in half and place them in a roasting pan. Season with salt and pepper, drizzle with the olive oil and cook for 8–10 minutes until golden brown.

For the pea and mint purée
1 Cook the peas in boiling salted water for 2–3 minutes. Drain and return to the pan. Add a little olive oil, mint, salt and pepper, then mash to a purée.

To serve
Arrange the fish, potatoes and pea purée on plates and serve with a sprig of parsley.

Duck Kebab
Karam Sethi | Trishna

If your only experience of a kebab is stumbling out of a pub and ordering meat on a stick, don't worry... Karam Sethi has an alternative version, packed with flavour that will linger in the memory rather than around your middle.

SERVES 2

For the coriander chutney
200g (7oz) fresh coriander leaves
1 green chilli
½ garlic clove
100g (3½oz) fresh root ginger
2 tbsp natural yogurt
1 tsp salt
1 tbsp lemon juice

For the duck kebabs
2 duck legs
1 green chilli, finely chopped
10g (¼oz) diced shallots
2 tbsp breadcrumbs
5g (⅛oz) finely diced fresh root ginger
5g (⅛oz) finely diced garlic
5g (⅛oz) chopped fresh coriander
½ tsp garam masala
2 tbsp vegetable oil
1 tomato, deseeded and sliced
¼ red onion, sliced
100g (3½oz) cucumber, julienned
juice of **1** lemon
2 pitta breads

For the coriander chutney
1 Blitz together all the coriander chutney ingredients in a food processor. Store the chutney in the refrigerator until ready to use.

For the duck kebab
1 Remove the meat from the duck legs and blitz it to a fine mince in a food processor.

2 Add the chilli, shallots, breadcrumbs, ginger, garlic, coriander and garam masala to the mince and mix well. Form 4 patties with the mince.

3 Heat the oil in a frying pan and cook the patties for 4 minutes on each side or until golden.

4 Meanwhile, combine the tomato, red onion slices, cucumber julienne and lemon juice to make a salad.

5 Toast the pitta breads. Cut them in half and spread some of the coriander chutney on the insides. Finally, add the salad and duck kebabs. Serve with a cold King Cobra lager (double fermented 8 per cent) as a reward for your healthy eating.

Chef's Tip
When the skin is removed from a duck leg, it is actually leaner than a skinless chicken leg. But if you aren't keen on duck, you can substitute lamb, chicken or venison for it.

Coconut and Galangal Soup with Prawns
Matthew Albert | Nahm

This fresh and delicious soup by Matthew Albert uses coconut as its main ingredient, so it is rich in fibre, vitamins and minerals. The recipe uses prawns, but you could use poached chicken instead, if you prefer.

SERVES 2

475ml (16fl oz) chicken stock
250ml (8fl oz) coconut milk
250ml (8fl oz) homemade
  coconut cream (*see* method)
pinch of salt
a little palm sugar
2 coriander roots
2–3 bird's eye chillies, to taste,
  plus an extra 4–5 bruised
3 stalks lemon grass, trimmed
  but left whole
3 red shallots, peeled
80g (3oz) galangal, peeled
  and sliced
3 kaffir lime leaves
100g (3½oz) wild mushrooms
150g (5oz) raw prawns, peeled
2–3 tbsp fish sauce
1 tbsp fresh lime juice
1 tbsp fresh coriander leaves

For the coconut cream

1   Take a coconut, place in your palm and crack it open with the back of a heavy knife or meat cleaver and discard the water inside.

2   Remove the flesh from the shell. Tap the outside to help loosen and release it. Rinse to remove any traces of the rusk.

3   Finely slice the coconut in preparation for a food processor. Blend until fine.

4   Add boiling water until submerged and blend for a further 2 minutes. Place muslin cloth over a non-metallic bowl and pour the mixture in.

5   Squeeze the cloth to release the milk into the bowl. Discard the flesh.

6   Leave the milk to stand for 20–30 minutes to allow the cream to float to the top. Skim off with a ladle and discard the water.

For the soup

1   In a large saucepan, combine stock with the coconut milk and cream. Simmer. Add a pinch of salt and palm sugar.

2   Bruise the coriander roots, 2–3 bird's eye chillies, lemon grass and shallots. Add to the stock with the galangal and lime leaves. Simmer for 5 minutes, then add the mushrooms and prawns. Simmer until the prawns turn pink and are cooked.

3   In a serving bowl, mix the fish sauce, lime juice, extra chillies and coriander leaves. Ladle in the soup and taste – it should be rich, salty, sour and hot. Poached chicken works well, too.

Salmon Daikon Roll
Ian Pengelley | Gilgamesh

Ian Pengelley was brought up in Hong Kong and has cooked throughout Asia. For *GQ*, he created a fresh and simple sushi roll using daikon, an Oriental white radish commonly known as mooli.

SERVES 2

1 large daikon (Japanese radish; or use ordinary radish), peeled and cut into 8cm (3¼in) chunks
200g (7oz) fresh salmon, cut into 10 x 2cm (4 x ¾in) strips
1 avocado, cut into 10cm (4in) long batons
1 red pepper, roasted, peeled, and cut into 10cm (4in) long batons
1 pickled radish (or use pickled cucumber), cut into 10cm (4in) long batons
1 bunch of mizuna (a Japanese leaf) or use mixed salad leaves

For the sauce
50ml (2fl oz) chive oil
100g (3½oz) mayonnaise
50ml (2fl oz) mirin (or use white wine)

For the sauce

1 Mix together all the sauce ingredients and set aside.

For the rolls

1 Slice the daikon chunks into thin slices using a mandolin.

2 Place salmon, avocado, pepper, pickled radish and leaves across the sheets of daikon, leaving a little of the ingredients sticking out at each end. Roll up each sheet tightly.

3 Slice a roll in two, stand the halves up on a plate. Cut the other roll(s) into 1cm (½in) pieces.

4 Arrange the smaller pieces on the plate around the half pieces, then dot a little sauce on the plate. Serve garnished with pea shoots, pickled ginger and purple shiso leaves, and serve with a bowl of sauce on the side.

Tartare de Boeuf
Daniel Boulud | Bar Boulud

One of those classic dishes that divides opinion, steak tartare is finely chopped or minced raw beef, carefully seasoned and served with an egg yolk. Most chefs have their own unique version, but Daniel Boulud's is one of the best in the world.

**SERVES 8 as a starter
or 4 for a main course**

For the mustard egg dressing
2 large eggs
15ml (½fl oz) Orleans mustard
15ml (½fl oz) Dijon mustard
15ml (½fl oz) Sherry vinegar
175ml (6fl oz) grapeseed oil
60ml (2¼fl oz) olive oil
Tabasco
salt and freshly ground
  white pepper

For the steak tartare
100g (3½oz) finely chopped
  red onion
800g (1lb 12oz) beef sirloin
50g (1¾oz) finely chopped
  cornichon
50g (1¾oz) finely chopped capers
1 tsp chopped anchovies
30g (1oz) Dijon mustard
¼ bunch of flat leaf parsley,
  chopped
¼ bunch of chives, finely sliced
Worcestershire sauce
tomato ketchup
salt and freshly ground white
  pepper
100g (3½oz) pasteurized egg yolks
10g (¼oz) Dijon mustard

> **Chef's Tip**
> You can place the sirloin in the freezer for 20 minutes to firm – which can aid in slicing and chopping neat dice – but do not freeze it.

For the mustard egg dressing

1 Bring a small pot of water to the boil. Gently slip in the eggs and cook for 3 minutes. Remove the eggs from the pot and cool under cold running water for 2 minutes.

2 Crack the eggs in half and scoop the insides into a blender with the mustards and vinegar and whir together. Slowly drizzle in the oils, then add some Tabasco and seasoning. Blend until the dressing is light and fluffy, then refrigerate it until you are ready to serve.

For the steak tartare

1 Bring a small pot of water to the boil. Add the finely chopped onion and simmer for 30 seconds. Strain and pat dry.

2 You can use minced beef, but I prefer dicing it. On a chopping board, using a very sharp knife, cut the beef into 5mm (¼in) thick slices, then cut the slices into thin ribbons. Slice the ribbons crossways to make fine dice. Transfer the meat to a large bowl with the onion, cornichon, capers, anchovies, mustard, parsley and chives and toss to combine. Season with Worcestershire sauce, ketchup, salt and pepper.

3 In a small bowl, whisk together the yolk and mustard, then season to taste with salt and pepper.

4 If serving the tartare as a starter, divide it into 8 equal portions. If serving as a main course, divide it into 4 equal portions. Arrange one portion in the middle of a chilled plate in the shape of a patty. Form a 2.5cm (1in) diameter shallow well in the centre of the patty and fill this with the mustard egg dressing. Spoon a dot of egg yolk mix in the centre to mimic the look of a fried egg.

Poached and Roasted Foie Gras
Jean Denis Le Bras | Sketch

'It is not complicated, but it does use a lot of produce,' says Jean Denis Le Bras, who developed this dish in conjunction with the legendary Pierre Gagnaire. 'You will need to prepare the 'sketchup' and the consommé the day before, but the assembly is easy and the end result, well worth it.'

SERVES 4

400g (14oz) (1 lobe) fresh foie gras
5g (⅛oz) fine salt
2g (1/16oz) freshly ground black pepper
1g (¼ tsp) sugar
500g (1lb 2oz) Ratte potatoes
1 Thai grapefruit, segmented
1 candy beetroot, thinly sliced

For the sketchup
oil, for frying
400g (14oz) raw beetroot, diced
100g (3½oz) carrot, diced
100g (3½oz) red pepper, diced
100g (3½oz) white onions, diced
1 stalk of lemon grass
1 garlic clove
20g (¾oz) fresh root ginger
75ml (2½fl oz) vegetable stock
75ml (2½fl oz) Xérès vinegar
salt and freshly ground black pepper

For the hibiscus consommé
1 litre (1¾ pints) water
30g (1oz) lemon grass
30g (1oz) honey
5g (⅛oz) salt
40g (1½oz) dried hibiscus flowers

1 Season the foie gras with salt, pepper and sugar, then leave it to marinate for 4 hours.

2 To make the sketchup, heat a little oil and pan-fry the vegetables in a large pot with the lemon grass, garlic and ginger, then add the vegetable stock. Once reduced, add the Xérès vinegar and cook until the beetroot has completely softened. Blend to a purée and season to taste. Set aside.

3 Next make the hibiscus consommé: Bring all the ingredients, except the hibiscus flowers, slowly to the boil. Once at boiling point, add the hibiscus flowers. Cover the pan with clingfilm and leave to infuse for 2 hours, then pass the mixture through a fine sieve. Set aside.

4 To make the garnish, boil the whole potatoes, then peel and slice them. Preheat the oven to 150°C/fan 130°C/300°F/gas mark 2.

5 Roast the whole lobe of foie gras in a very hot pan for 15 seconds on each side, then place it on a baking tray and oven cook for 10 minutes. Once cooked, gently poach the foie gras in the hibiscus consommé for 4 minutes at 85°C/185°F. Take out the foie gras and cut it into 4 large slices, then season with black pepper.

6 Mix the grapefruit and sketchup together and arrange it on the plate. Add a layer of potato slices, then place the foie gras on top and garnish with the raw beetroot slices.

Artichoke Tortellini
Heinz Beck | Apsleys

Sensational and simple, this tortellini lets the ingredients speak for themselves, so make sure you go for Sardinian artichokes. Filling the tortellini really isn't as fiddly as you might think. This dish works wonderfully as a starter or a main course.

SERVES 4

For the tortellini pasta dough
160g (5¾oz) '00' flour
85g (3oz) semolina
3 egg yolks
pinch of salt

For the filling
250g (9oz) cherry tomatoes
extra virgin olive oil
salt and freshly ground black pepper
chopped thyme
300g (10½oz) globe artichokes, trimmed
1 garlic clove, finely chopped
pinch of chilli flakes
400g (14oz) buffalo ricotta cheese
3g (¹⁄₁₀oz) fresh mint, chopped

For the Sardinian artichoke and tomato sauce
2kg (4lb 8oz) Sardinian artichokes, trimmed
100g (3½oz) cherry tomatoes
extra virgin olive oil
fresh basil leaves
1 garlic clove, peeled
1 red chilli

1 Pour the flour and semolina into a mound on a clean work surface and make a well in the centre. Add the egg yolks and a pinch of salt and mix with your hands to form a dough. Add a little water if required and knead until the dough is soft, then put into a bowl, cover with clingfilm and let it rest for a day in a cool place.

2 Wash the cherry tomatoes and affect the skin with a small cross-shaped cut. Put them into boiling water for a few seconds, then drain and cool in iced water. Peel the tomatoes, cut into quarters and remove the seeds. Put the flesh in a bowl: dress with extra virgin olive oil, salt and thyme and let stand for 30 minutes.

3 Tip the tomatoes on to a baking tray lined with baking paper and let them dry in the oven at 80°C/ fan 60°C/176°F/gas mark ⅛ for 4 hours. Chop the dried tomatoes, then leave to cool.

4 Clean the globe artichokes. Slice a quarter of the artichokes and dice the rest, then sauté them in a hot pan with a little oil, garlic and a pinch of chilli flakes. Mix the cooked artichokes and dried tomatoes together with the ricotta and chopped mint to make a purée and season to taste.

5 Roll the pasta dough into a long wide strip about 1mm thick, either by hand or using a machine. Cut the strip into thin rectangles. Pipe a little filling on half of each rectangle, then fold the dough over the filling and seal each parcel by hand. Repeat until the filling is used up. Set them aside while you make the sauce.

For the Sardinian artichoke and tomato sauce
1 Clean and dice the Sardinian artichokes, then fry in a hot pan. Set aside.

2 Boil the cherry tomatoes and remove their skins as above, then cut the flesh into quarters and remove the seeds. Process the tomato flesh in a blender, then pass through a strainer and dress with extra virgin olive oil. Pour the tomato sauce into a sterilized glass jar. Add the basil leaves, garlic clove and whole chilli pepper. Seal the jar and cook in a water bath for 2 hours. Once cooked, remove and discard the basil, garlic and whole chilli, then process again in a blender with the cooked artichokes until smooth.

3 Cook the tortellini in boiling salted water until al dente (about 3–4 minutes). Portion the sauce on to 4 warmed plates, adding the tortellini on top. Serve with freshly shaved or grated Parmesan.

Risotto of Wild Mushroom
John Campbell | The Vineyard, Stockcross

This wild mushroom risotto might look complicated, but the beauty of John Campbell's recipe is that you can prepare the two mushroom elements (the purée and the stock) in advance. That makes the final dish a doddle to dish up.

SERVES 4–6

For the cep purée
25g (1oz) onion, finely sliced
5g (⅛oz) dried ceps
5g (⅛oz) butter
1 bay leaf
1g fresh thyme
¼ garlic clove
40ml (1½fl oz) Noilly Prat
30g (1oz) button mushrooms, finely sliced
30g (1oz) field mushrooms, finely sliced
100ml (3½fl oz) chicken stock
30ml (1fl oz) cream
salt and freshly ground black pepper

For the mushroom nage
50g (1¾oz) onions, sliced
15g (½oz) butter
3g (⅒oz) thyme
4 bay leaves
250g (9oz) field mushrooms, sliced
500g (1lb 2oz) whole button mushrooms
2 litres (3½ pints) water
15g (½oz) dried ceps

For the risotto
50g (1¾oz) shallots, diced
25ml (¾fl oz) vegetable oil
200g (7oz) carnaroli rice
1 litre (1¾ pints) mushroom nage (*see above*)
75g (2½oz) mixed wild mushrooms
50g (1¾oz) butter
salt and freshly ground black pepper
10g (¼oz) Parmesan cheese, grated
5g (⅛oz) chives, chopped
sherry vinegar

For the cep purée
1 Colour the onion and ceps in the butter with the herbs and garlic for 5 minutes. Add the Noilly Prat and reduce completely. Add the mushrooms and cook for 15 minutes. Pour in the stock and reduce it by two-thirds. Now add the cream, reduce it by half, then blitz the mixture in a blender until smooth. Season to taste. Set aside.

For the mushroom nage
1 Caramelize the onions in the butter with the herbs, then add the field mushrooms. Sweat them down until dry, then add the button mushrooms. When all the water is released from the mushrooms and a good colour is achieved, pour in the water and bring to the boil. Reduce the heat and simmer for 30 minutes, then remove from the heat, add the dried ceps and infuse for 10 minutes. Set aside.

For the risotto
1 Sweat the shallots in the oil for 2 minutes, ensuring they don't colour. Add the rice and sweat for a further minute. Pour in the nage a little at a time, stirring constantly, until the rice is nearly cooked, which will take around 15 minutes.

2 In a separate pan, sauté the mushrooms in the butter, then add the rice. Incorporate more nage as required. Season with salt and pepper.

3 Add the Parmesan, chives and sherry vinegar to taste, then 100g (3½oz) cep purée. The consistency should neither be too loose, nor too wet. Adjust this using the nage. Serve the risotto in bowls and garnish as required (I use fresh chervil and some freshly sliced Périgord truffle).

Lobster Mango Salad
Michel Roux Jnr | Le Gavroche

Cooking with lobster always guarantees the wow factor, and this beautiful supper (or starter) will mark you out as a kitchen superstar. With a perfect mix of textures, tastes and colours, the end result should look almost too good to eat... almost.

SERVES 2

140g (5oz) caster sugar
rind of ½ lime, cut into thin
  julienne
1 x 500–600g (1lb 2oz–1lb 5oz)
  cooked lobster
½ ripe but firm mango, peeled
  and diced
½ avocado, diced
1 spring onion, sliced
salt
juice of **1** lime
6 basil leaves, torn
2 tbsp extra virgin olive oil
green Tabasco
endive leaves and mixed salad
  leaves, to serve (optional)

1 Dissolve the sugar in 125ml (4fl oz) water in a pan over a medium heat. Add the lime rind and simmer for gently for 5 minutes. Drain and leave to cool.

2 Cut the lobster tail meat into medallions and dice the rest of the meat.

3 Put the lobster meat in a bowl with the mango, avocado, spring onion, seasoning, lime juice, basil, olive oil, green Tabasco and the lime rind. Very gently toss the salad. Serve in glass bowls or spoon the mixture onto endive leaves. Dress with the remaining sauce and serve with mixed leaves.

Chef's Tip
Prawns or crab meat can be used instead of lobster if you are on a budget. And don't forget – everything can be prepped in advance and assembled at the very last moment.

Sicilian Rabbit
Francesco Mazzei | L'Anima

Francesco Mazzei is one of the brightest stars on the London restaurant scene and this brilliant, gutsy and delicious one-pot recipe captures all the flavours of the Italian countryside.

SERVES 4

1 rabbit (around 1.3kg), cut into 16 similar-sized pieces
plain flour, for dusting
olive oil
70g (2½oz) celery, chopped
70g (2½oz) fennel, chopped
70g (2½oz) onions, chopped
50g (1¾oz) shallots, chopped
10g (¼oz) garlic, chopped
80g (3oz) Chantenay carrots, chopped
5g (⅛oz) fennel seeds
500ml (18fl oz) red wine vinegar
20g (¾oz) muscovado sugar
20g (¾oz) tomato paste
1.3 litres (2¼ pints) rabbit stock
70g (2½oz) taggiasche olives
20g (¾oz) sultanas
5g (⅛oz) fresh marjoram, chopped
1 sprig of thyme
5g (⅛oz) pine nuts
10g (¼oz) sun-dried tomatoes

To serve
5g (⅛oz) pistachios, crushed
15ml (½fl oz) olive oil

1 Dust the rabbit pieces with flour, then brown them in a pan with a little olive oil. Set aside.

2 Sauté the celery, fennel, onions, shallots, garlic and carrots with the fennel seeds until caramelized.

3 Add the red wine vinegar, sugar and tomato paste and simmer until the liquid is reduced.

4 Add the rabbit pieces and the stock and simmer gently for 20 minutes.

5 When the rabbit is cooked through, add the olives, sultanas, marjoram, thyme, pine nuts and tomatoes. Serve the rabbit with crushed pistachios and a few drops of olive oil on top.

Chef's Tip
Another method for preparing rabbit is to confit, which will keep the meat even more tender. Cover the rabbit with olive oil, garlic cloves, rosemary and thyme and cook in the oven at 80°C for 4 hours.

Tomato and Chilli Pasta with Prawns
Giorgio Locatelli | Locanda Locatelli

The Don of Italian cooking, Giorgio Locatelli is an inspirational and innovative chef, beloved by celebrities and serious foodies alike. This recipe for *paccheri con gamberi* is the perfect balance of fresh seafood and subtle heat.

SERVES 4

3 tomatoes
extra virgin olive oil
2 garlic cloves, chopped
1 red chilli, deseeded and finely chopped
1 green chilli, deseeded and finely chopped
16 peeled tiger prawns, cut into thirds (reserve the heads and shells)
8 peeled tiger prawns, with heads
salt and freshly ground black pepper
1½ glasses of white wine
400g (14oz) paccheri pasta
handful of flat leaf parsley, finely chopped (reserve the stalks)

For the stock
1 tbsp olive oil
½ carrot, cut into chunks
½ onion, cut into chunks
1 celery stick, cut into chunks
reserved parsley stalks (*see* above)
1 garlic clove
1 bay leaf
2 black peppercorns
reserved prawn heads and shells (*see* above)
½ **tbsp** tomato paste

> *Chef's Tip*
> For each 100g (3 ½oz) pasta, use 1 litre (1¾ pints) water (and 5–8g/ ⅛– ¼oz salt) to allow the pasta to keep moving so it cooks evenly. Taste it regularly to avoid overcooking.

For the stock

1 Heat the olive oil in a pan. Add the vegetables, parsley stalks, garlic, bay leaf and peppercorns. Sweat to soften, but not to colour.

2 Add the prawn heads and shells to the pan and cook until they turn bright red. Add the tomato paste and cook over a low heat for 2 minutes. Add water to cover the ingredients and bring to the boil, then reduce the heat and simmer for 15 minutes. Pass the ingredients through a fine sieve and set aside.

For the pasta and sauce

1 Get a large pan of boiling, salted water ready for the pasta. Blanch the tomatoes for 10 seconds, then run them under cold water and peel them. Cut the tomatoes in half and scoop out the seeds, then cut each into 2 or 4 pieces and set aside.

2 Heat some olive oil in a sauté pan. Put in the garlic and cook it gently until it colours, then add the chillies. Incorporate the prawns and cook for 1 minute, crushing the heads at the same time. Season, add the white wine and allow the alcohol to evaporate. Add the stock and reserved tomato petals and reduce the heat.

3 Cook the pasta for 6 minutes, drain it and add it to the pan containing the prawns. Continue cooking the pasta in the sauce for 2 more minutes so that it soaks up some of the liquid. Finish by adding 2 tablespoons extra virgin olive oil and the chopped parsley.

Norwegian Red King Crab Risotto
Pascal Proyart | One-O-One

One of London's top seafood chefs, Pascal Proyart, describes the star ingredient in his recipe as the king of shellfish. 'It may be tricky to get hold of,' he says, 'but once you have experienced the flavour, you will never, ever forget it.'

SERVES 4

For the candied tomato
4 large ripe plum tomatoes
1 tsp olive oil
salt and rock sea salt
ground white peppercorns
pinch of caster sugar
1 garlic clove, sliced
leaves from **2** sprigs of lemon thyme

For the pancake
400ml (14fl oz) full-fat milk
3 eggs
1 tsp grated Parmesan cheese
salt and freshly ground black pepper

For the sauce
40ml (1½fl oz) light crab bisque
100g (3½oz) unsalted butter
1 tsp black truffle oil

For the risotto
150ml (5½fl oz) light crab bisque
100g (3½oz) light chicken stock
3 tsp olive oil
2 tsp chopped shallot
2 garlic cloves, chopped
150g (5½oz) arborio risotto rice
30ml (1fl oz) white wine
2 tsp whipped cream
20g (¾oz) grated Parmesan cheese
1 tsp black truffle oil
1 tsp chopped flat leaf parsley
1 tsp chopped fresh tarragon

To finish
50g (1¾oz) butter
4 x 100g (3½oz) royal king crab legs
5g (⅛oz) shavings of Parmesan cheese
artisan salad leaves
salt and freshly ground black pepper

1 Preheat the oven to 90°C/fan 70°C/195°F/ gas mark ¼. Blanch the tomatoes in boiling water for 6–8 seconds, then place in iced water. Peel them, cut each in half and deseed. Lay a sheet of baking paper on a baking sheet. Drizzle on the oil and sprinkle with salt, pepper and sugar. Add the tomatoes, brush with the olive oil, season with more salt, pepper and sugar. Top with garlic slices and lemon thyme. Bake for 3 hours until the tomatoes are semi-dry but moist. Put the tomatoes and their cooking juice in a container and set aside.

2 Mix the pancake ingredients in a bowl and season. Warm a nonstick pan and cook the batter over a low heat for 2 minutes. Cut the pancake into 4 round shapes and gently remove from the pan. Wrap in baking paper and set aside.

3 Heat the crab bisque in a pan and bring to the boil, then add the butter and truffle oil. Blend with a hand blender – the sauce should be frothy, like a cappuccino. Set aside in a warm place.

For the risotto

1 Add the crab bisque and stock to a casserole and bring to a gentle boil. Heat the oil in a casserole, add the shallot and garlic and sweat *à blanc* (there should be no colour on them). Add the rice and 'pearl' well (lightly toss in olive oil until it turns translucent) for 1 minute. Add the wine and cook gently, stirring, until it is absorbed. Add the warm stock and cook for 15 minutes, stirring, until the rice is flaky. Mix in the cream, grated Parmesan, truffle oil and herbs.

2 Prepare a little beurre noisette by melting the butter in a pan until golden and bubbling. Set aside.

3 Take each crab leg and, with scissors, cut the shell but not the meat. Remove the meat and cut it into cannon shapes (2–3 per leg). Warm the tomatoes, crab meat and pancakes in a low oven for 2–3 minutes. Place 2 candied tomatoes in the middle of each plate, lay on a pancake and top with 2 tablespoons of risotto. Fold the pancake over the rice in a half-moon shape. Place 2 crab canons alongside. Add Parmesan and salad leaves. Season. Warm the sauce, blend again, skim off the foam and drizzle it over the dish. Add a few drops of beurre noisette.

Honey and Cider Roast Leg of Lamb
Gordon Ramsay

When it comes to British Michelin-starred chefs, we could never ignore the foul-mouthed, fantastically talented and utterly unforgettable Gordon Ramsay. This roast leg of lamb is one of his most popular recipes and, once you've made it, you'll understand why.

SERVES 6

1 leg of lamb (about 2kg/4lb 8oz), fat trimmed, skin scored in a crisscross pattern
olive oil, to drizzle
salt and freshly ground black pepper
3–4 garlic cloves, unpeeled, halved
few sprigs of thyme
juice from ½ lemon
4 apples (Russets or Braeburns), sliced into quarters and cores cut out
500ml (18fl oz) medium cider
runny honey, to drizzle
300ml (½ pint) lamb or chicken stock

1 Preheat the oven to 220°C/fan 200°C/425°F/gas mark 7. Weigh the lamb and calculate the final cooking time at 12 minutes per 450g (1lb) for medium-rare, 15 minutes for medium.

2 Drizzle the lamb with olive oil, then rub all over with salt and pepper.

3 Place the joint in a deep roasting pan and scatter the garlic and thyme over and around. Pour over the lemon juice and drizzle again with olive oil. Sprinkle with a little more seasoning, then roast for 20 minutes.

4 Remove the lamb from the oven and reduce the heat to 180°C/fan 160°C/350°F/gas mark 4. Scatter the apples around the pan and baste the lamb with cider. Turn the meat over and drizzle with 2 tablespoons of honey.

5 Return the lamb on to the oven for 30 minutes. Turn it around, baste with the pan juices, then drizzle over another tablespoon of honey. Continue to roast for the calculated time. To check if it is done, insert a skewer into the thickest part of the lamb, then press lightly – the redder the juices are, the rarer the meat is.

6 Lift the lamb to a carving board and cover with foil. Rest it in a warm place while you prepare the gravy.

7 At this point, the apples and garlic in the roasting pan should be very soft. Press them with a fork, then tip the entire contents of the pan into a fine sieve over a saucepan. Push down with the back of a ladle to extract all the juices and flavour from the apples and garlic. Discard the pulp. Place the saucepan over a medium heat and add the stock. Bring to the boil and let it bubble vigorously until the sauce has thickened to a desired gravy consistency. Taste and adjust the seasoning, then pour the gravy into a warm serving jug.

8 Carve the lamb into thin slices and serve drizzled with the apple and cider gravy. Crisp roast potatoes and steamed tenderstem broccoli make the perfect accompaniments to this dish.

Beef, Cucumber, Raspberries, Nasturtium
Marcus Wareing | The Berkeley

This dish by Marcus Wareing is best created using a fantastic breed of Scottish beef called Galloway for a delicious pan-roasted fillet. The raspberries add acidity, while the nasturtium's unique peppery taste mirrors the classic horseradish.

SERVES 8

For the beef sauce
beef trimmings (*see* below) or
  a small piece of fatty meat
  such as brisket
1 shallot, cut into julienne
2 sprigs of thyme
1 bay leaf
5 white peppercorns
5 coriander seeds
500ml (18fl oz) port
1 litre (1¾ pints) red wine
1.7 litres (3 pints) chicken stock
1.7 litres (3 pints) veal or beef
  stock

For the raspberry sauce
1 punnet raspberries
2 tbsp raspberry vinegar

For the beef fillet
2 cucumbers
salt and freshly ground black
  pepper
2kg (4lb 8oz) beef fillet,
  trimmed of fat (reserve the fat)
  and portioned into 250g (9oz)
  pieces
2 tbsp oil
knob of butter
32 nasturtium leaves

For the beef sauce
1 Put the beef trimmings in a pan set over a medium heat until the fat begins to melt. Add the shallot, thyme, bay leaf, peppercorns and coriander seeds and allow them to colour. Strain to remove the beef trimmings and the aromatics from the pan and set these aside.

2 Deglaze the pan with the port and wine and reduce to a thick glaze.

3 Return the beef trimmings and shallot to the glaze. Add the chicken and veal or beef stock and simmer until the liquid is reduced by three-quarters, then strain again. Set aside.

For the raspberry sauce
1 Put 300ml (½ pint) of the beef sauce in a jug, add 8 raspberries and the raspberry vinegar. Set aside.

For the beef fillet
1 Cook the cucumbers for 2 minutes on a hot griddle pan, turning them as you cook.

2 Season the beef. Heat the oil in a pan, add the beef and cook for 4 minutes, turning after 2 minutes, to cook it medium-rare. Add a knob of butter to the pan for the final 30 seconds.

3 Cut the cucumber into quarters. Cut all of the remaining raspberries in half.

4 Plate each dish with a cooked cucumber quarter, some halved raspberries, 8 nasturtium leaves, a portion of beef and some of each of the sauces.

Chef's Tip
If you are looking to add an extra element, add some bone marrow that has simply been cooked in a hot pan for 30 seconds on each side.

ALFRESCO

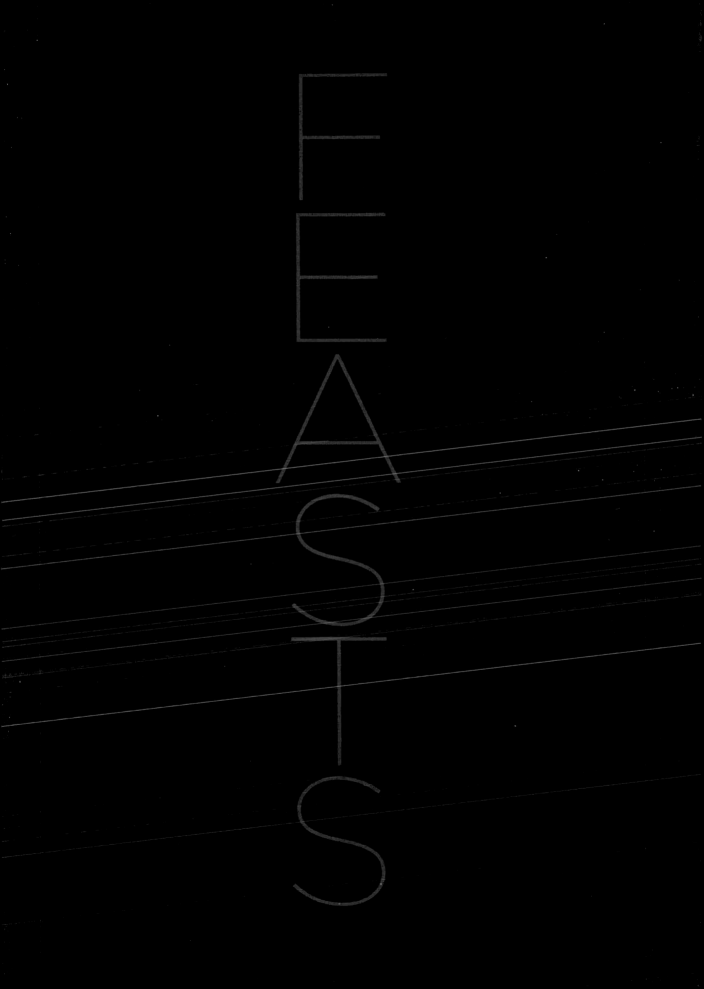

Thai Green Mango Salad with Grilled Chicken and Quinoa

Anthony Demetre | Les Deux Salons

Not so much a side salad as a meal in itself, this fresh and fruity combination of mangoes, chicken and quinoa with punchy Thai flavours will win over the lettuce lovers and the quiche dodgers.

SERVES 2

2 chicken breasts, skin removed

For the dressing
6 tbsp Squid Brand fish sauce
6 tbsp Kaffir lime juice
2 tbsp grated palm sugar
4 tbsp Thai chilli sauce
30g (1oz) red chilli, finely diced, or 3 pinches of dried chilli flakes
1 stalk of lemon grass, very finely sliced

For the salad
80g (3oz) cooked quinoa (do not overcook — make sure it remains a little crunchy)
100g (3½oz) fresh root ginger, peeled and cut into thin batons
100g (3½oz) unsalted peanuts, lightly toasted and roughly chopped
100g (3½oz) spring onions, thinly sliced
½ cucumber, peeled, halved, deseeded and thinly sliced
2 green mangoes, peeled and cut into thin strips
4 tbsp torn Thai basil
4 tbsp torn fresh mint leaves
4 tbsp torn fresh coriander leaves

For the garnish
4 tbsp toasted desiccated coconut
4 tbsp Thai onion flakes
grated rind of **3** Kaffir limes

For the dressing

1 Combine the dressing ingredients and correct the saltiness, sourness and bitterness to taste. Set aside for a minimum of 30 minutes. Place the chicken in a bowl. When the marinade has had time to infuse, add 4 tablespoons of it to the chicken and reserve the rest. Marinate the chicken overnight.

2 Next day, preheat the oven to 180°C/fan 160°C/350°F/gas mark 4. Take the chicken out of the marinade (discard this marinade), pat it dry and grill or fry the chicken until it is nicely browned all over. Place it in a roasting pan and cook it in the oven for about 8 minutes or until it is cooked through. Set aside to cool completely. Pour the cooking juices into the reserved dressing.

For the salad

1 Slice the cooled chicken into thin strips, put it into a mixing bowl, add all the salad ingredients and half of the dressing and mix together. Don't be too rough — you don't want the chicken to break up. Taste and add more dressing if desired.

To finish

Combine all the garnish ingredients, sprinkle the garnish over the salad and serve immediately.

Red Cabbage and Apple Salad
Raphael Duntoye | La Petite Maison

This brilliantly conceived salad delivers a combination of flavours (sweet, zingy and savoury) and textures (soft, chewy and crunchy) that will have your guests racing back to the bowl rather than the barbecue.

SERVES 1

For the salad
70g (2½oz) red cabbage, thinly sliced
7 orange segments
20g (¾oz) Pink Lady apple, cut into 1cm (½in) dice
10g (¼oz) golden raisins
5g (⅛oz) chopped hazelnuts
salt and freshly ground black pepper
5g (⅛oz) chives, snipped, to garnish

For the dressing
25ml (¾fl oz) orange juice
25ml (¾fl oz) white balsamic vinegar
7ml (⅛fl oz) sherry vinegar
25ml (¾fl oz) olive oil
37ml (1⅓fl oz) hazelnut oil
pinch of salt

Chef's Tip
Once you have made the salad, it is well worth leaving it in the refrigerator for 1–2 hours to help the flavours intensify.

1 Mix the red cabbage with the orange segments, apple pieces, golden raisins and chopped hazelnuts. Season to taste.

2 Mix the dressing ingredients together and dress the salad.

3 Garnish the salad with chopped chives to serve.

Cured Tuna Salad with Fennel
Nick Bell | Bocca di Lupo

This lightly cured tuna recipe works brilliantly because the fennel and orange dressing does not overpower the delicate flavour of the fish, but gives the dish a light and fresh finish.

SERVES 4

1 fennel bulb
1 blood orange
handful of mizuna or rocket leaves
½ red onion, thinly sliced on a mandolin
4 cherry vine tomatoes, each sliced into 6 pieces
salt and freshly ground black pepper
200g (7oz) cured tuna, very thinly sliced
2 tbsp good-quality olive oil

For the olive oil dressing
100ml (3½fl oz) light olive oil
100ml (3½fl oz) extra virgin olive oil
75ml (2½fl oz) white wine vinegar

1 Pick off the shoots from the fennel tips and coarsly chop them (alternatively, you can use a pinch of chopped dill), then set aside. Thinly slice the fennel from the root end and place the slices in iced water until crisp, then drain them and pat dry.

2 Segment and dice the blood orange and retain any juice from the centre.

3 Mix all the olive oil dressing ingredients together and set aside.

4 Place a small handful of fennel slices and the mizuna or rocket leaves in a mixing bowl. Add a large pinch of the sliced red onion and around 3 tablespoons diced blood orange and some of the orange juice. Add the equivalent of 4 sliced tomatoes and a large pinch of fennel shoots or dill. Season with salt and pepper and add the olive oil dressing. Mix everything together and place a small handful of the salad in the centre of each plate. Lay slices of tuna around the salad, so that they overlap slightly.

5 To make the final dressing, combine a spoonful of diced blood orange, 2 tablespoons blood orange juice and the olive oil. Add a small pinch of fennel shoots or dill. Mix well and use to dress the tuna, giving 5–6 pieces of orange to each plate.

Vegetarian Skewer
Oliver Peyton

'There are two problems with most barbecues,' says Oliver Peyton. 'The first is that they only really cater to carnivores. And the second is that they don't really give you enough space to cook anything.' Peyton's solution to both problems can be found in this recipe for vegetable skewers, which are brought to life by a fresh and flavourful chive oil dressing.

SERVES 4

For the chive oil
1 bunch of fresh chives, roughly chopped
50ml (2fl oz) rapeseed oil
salt

For the skewers
8 asparagus tips, including one-third of the stalks
salt
8 spring onions, trimmed
1 yellow or green courgette, cut into 8 wedges
1 red pepper, cut into 8 wedges
1 red onion, cut into 8 wedges
8 cherry tomatoes
pinch of cayenne pepper
knob of butter

1   First make the chive oil. In a small blender, blitz the chives with the oil and a pinch of salt. Pass the mixture through a fine-meshed sieve, then set aside.

2   Plunge the asparagus into a saucepan of salted boiling water, bring the water back to the boil and cook for 30 seconds. Lift out the asparagus with a slotted spoon and plunge it into a bowl of iced water. Drop the spring onions into the boiling water, then lift them out as soon as it comes back to the boil. Do the same with the courgette, allowing 45 seconds in the water, followed by the red pepper and red onion, allowing 30 seconds each and immersing them in iced water after blanching.

3   Drain the vegetables. Thread the blanched vegetables and the tomatoes onto skewers, folding the spring onions in half as you thread them on. Place the skewers on a tray. Prepare and light the barbecue.

4   Bring 1 tablespoon of water to the boil in a small saucepan with the cayenne and a pinch of salt. Remove from the heat and whisk in the butter. Brush this mixture over the vegetables. Place the skewers on the barbecue and cook for 7–8 minutes on each side until the vegetables are lightly charred. Serve, hot or cold, with the chive oil.

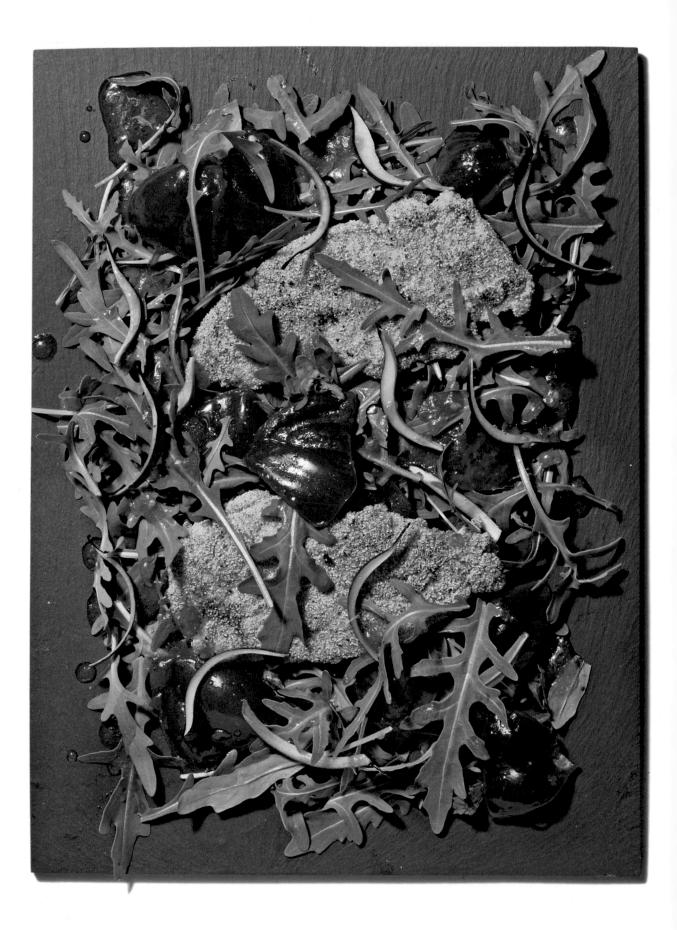

Crispy Chicken Salad
Simon Schama

This combination of crispy, thin, cornmeal-coated slice of chicken breast, on top of tomatoes that have been rendering their juices for hours, with green toasty rocket, is a marriage made in heaven.

SERVES 4

For the salad
1kg (2lb 4oz) ripe, large, field-grown tomatoes
juice of **2** lemons
salt and freshly ground black pepper
2 garlic cloves, crushed
220ml (8fl oz) extra virgin olive oil
6 handfuls of rocket (as fresh as possible)
1 red onion, sliced

For the chicken
400g (14oz) coarse yellow cornmeal or polenta
1 tbsp good-quality chilli powder
2 tbsp smoked Spanish paprika
3 eggs, beaten
2 boneless chicken breasts, thinly sliced and beaten with the flat side of a meat tenderizer under baking paper or clingfilm until almost transparent
2 tbsp olive oil

For the salad
1 Halve, deseed and core the tomatoes. Place the cores and pulp into a large mesh sieve set over a bowl and press it through with the back of a wooden spoon, rendering just the juice into the bowl. Cut the flesh of the halved tomatoes into small cubes and drop it into the bowl.

2 Add the lemon juice, salt and pepper, crushed garlic and, little by little, the olive oil to the tomato. Let the tomato salad sit at room temperature (never put tomatoes in the fridge) for a couple of hours, stirring it occasionally. Half an hour before serving, toss the rocket and onion with the tomato and mix well.

For the chicken
1 Mix the cornmeal or polenta with the chilli and paprika in a bowl. Place a bowl of the beaten eggs alongside it. Dredge the thin chicken slices, one by one, in the spiced cornmeal, shake off the excess coating, then dip them in the egg and dredge again, ensuring the cornmeal and egg cling to the meat.

2 Film a large nonstick frying pan with the olive oil and set it over a high heat. Place the coated chicken pieces in the pan and reduce the heat to medium-high. Leave them alone for 3 minutes, then carefully turn them with a spatula and repeat. Try not to overcrowd your pan. If necessary, set the chicken on a plate lined with kitchen paper, but they shouldn't be especially greasy. Serve immediately, accompanied with the salad.

Razor Clams with Chorizo, Wild Garlic Crust and Crisp Garlic
Oliver Peyton

It is always best to try to purchase your razor clams still alive and cook them on the day you buy them. This tasty, succulent shellfish has a texture a little like that of a squid, which is why this recipe with chorizo and garlic works so well.

SERVES 4

salted butter
20ml (⅔fl oz) good-quality olive oil
1 banana shallot, sliced
few sprigs of thyme
8 very alive razor clams, rinsed in cold water to remove any grit
glug of white wine
2 cooking chorizo sausages
oil, for frying
50g (1¾oz) wild garlic, thinly sliced (reserve the leaves)
handful of flat leaf parsley leaves
200g (7oz) panko breadcrumbs
salt and freshly ground black pepper
1 lemon

1   Put a knob of butter, the olive oil, shallot and thyme in a pan and heat fiercely. Throw in the clams and your white wine and cover. Cook for 1 minute, then take the pan off the heat. Discard any clams that do not open or that have damaged shells. Strain the cooking liquor and set it aside.

2   Take the clams out of their shells, slice the clam meat and set aside. Wash the clam shells and save them for the presentation of the dish.

3   Slice 1 chorizo sausage to very small dice and the other in very thin slices. Heat some oil in a pan and fry the sliced chorizo and garlic slices in separate batches until crispy, then drain on kitchen paper and set aside. Keep the oil hot and fry the parsley leaves very quickly until crisp.

4   For the herb crust, blitz your panko crumbs with 125g (4oz) of the butter, seasoning and the wild garlic leaves with their stalks removed.

5   Preheat the grill to a medium setting. Fry the chorizo cubes lightly, add the sliced clam meat, a squeeze of lemon juice and a little of the reserved clam cooking liquor. When hot, spoon the mixture into the empty clam shells, top with the crumb and place under the grill until golden. Serve the filled shells immediately on some more crumbs to hold them on the plate, scattered with fried parsley, chorizo and garlic.

Chef's Tip
For a quick sauce, heat the clam liquor with some butter, a squeeze of lemon, chopped tomato and seasoning.

Open Ciabatta of Egg and Crab Mayonnaise
Robert Thompson |
The Hambrough Restaurant

For a thoroughly modern and outrageously tasty version of that boring back-garden basic egg mayonnaise, try Robert Thompson's irresistible version with crab, asparagus and rocket. This recipe is so good, you don't even need to make your own mayo.

SERVES 4

1 ciabatta loaf
150g (5½fl oz) mayonnaise
100g (3½oz) brown crab meat, picked
juice of **1** lemon
salt and freshly ground black pepper
8 free-range organic eggs, hard-boiled and chopped
12 asparagus spears, blanched and refreshed in iced water
100g (3½oz) white crab meat, picked
handful of rocket
olive oil

1 Cut 4 thick slices from the ciabatta loaf and toast them lightly on each side (a griddle pan gives a really nice effect).

2 Combine the mayonnaise and the brown crab meat in a food processor. Blend until smooth, adding some of the lemon juice and seasoning to taste. Add the eggs and mix gently, then check the seasoning and adjust if necessary.

3 Spread each piece of ciabatta with a generous layer of egg mayonnaise. Top with the asparagus, white crab meat and rocket and finish with a little olive oil, pepper and more lemon juice.

Ratatouille
Heston Blumenthal | The Hinds Head

For a taste of the Mediterranean, this version of ratatouille is rich and distinctive. As Heston Blumenthal told *GQ*, 'The flavours of these vegetables in tomato fondue are far more evocative of long, warm summer evenings than a badly grilled burger.'

SERVES 4

**For the tomato fondue
(makes 1 litre/1¾ pints)**
3 medium onions, finely chopped
4 garlic cloves, roughly chopped
1 star anise, broken up
4 cloves
1 heaped tsp coriander seeds
250ml (9fl oz) olive oil
2.5kg (5lb 8oz) tomatoes, peeled, deseeded (reserve the juice from the seeds) and finely chopped
1 large bouquet garni (made with thyme, celery, leek, parsley and a bay leaf)
few drops of Worcestershire sauce
60ml (2¼fl oz) sherry vinegar
few drops drops of Tabasco
a little lemon rind, finely grated
1 tbsp tomato ketchup
salt

For the tomato ratatouille
3 medium aubergines
3 medium courgettes
1 head of fennel
2 red peppers
extra virgin olive oil
salt and freshly ground black pepper
3 tsp fresh thyme leaves
10 black olives, pitted and finely chopped
10 basil leaves, finely sliced
10 coriander seeds
oil, from the fried vegetables

For the tomato fondue
1 In a heavy-based casserole, gently sweat the onions, garlic and spices in the oil for 15 minutes. Add the tomatoes and reserved juice, the bouquet garni and the Worcestershire sauce. Bring to the boil, then simmer for 30 minutes.

2 Add the sherry vinegar, Tabasco, lemon rind, tomato ketchup and salt, then cover the pan and leave on a low heat for at least 3 hours. Check it occasionally to ensure it isn't burning. When it is ready, it will be dark red and have a thick, jam-like consistency. Remove the bouquet garni and spices before mixing the fondue with the tomato ratatouille (*see* below).

For the tomato ratatouille
1 Top and tail the aubergines and courgettes. Stand each vegetable upright and slice down the edges, removing the skin and about 3mm (⅛in) of flesh. (Discard the inner sections, or use them in another dish.) Trim each slice into a rectangle, then cut these into strips about 3mm (⅛in) thick. Bunch together the strips and cut across the lengths, leaving you with 3mm (⅛in) cubes. Set aside. Preheat the grill on a high setting.

2 Cut the top and bottom off the fennel and remove the outer layers, leaving V-shaped pieces of fennel. Cut them in half so that you are left with two slightly curved pieces. Trim and cut these as as you did the other vegetables.

3 Remove the stalk, pith and seeds from the red peppers, rub them with olive oil and place them, skin-side up, under the grill until they go black all over. Peel them and dice the flesh as above.

4 Heat a large frying pan and add 2mm (⅟₁₆in) of olive oil. When hot, add the aubergines in one layer. Cook for 3 minutes, then tip into a fine mesh sieve, allowing the juice to drain into a bowl. Season and add ½ teaspoon of thyme leaves. Set aside. Using fresh olive oil, repeat the process with the courgettes on a slightly lower heat and cooking for 2 minutes. Set aside. Finally, cook the fennel for 5–6 minutes. Drain as before. To finish the dish, mix together all the vegetables, the olives, basil, coriander seeds and remaining thyme, then add to the tomato fondue.

5 Finally, mix in a little oil from the fried vegetables to your taste, season and serve. If you want to eat this hot, reheat it in a moderate oven for 5 minutes.

Jellied Eel and Ham Hock Terrine
Claude Bosi | Hibiscus

Nothing could be more indicative of an English summer than jellied eels and ham hock. And who do we have to thank for combining these two ingredients into a stunning terrine? A Frenchman, of course. *Sacré bleu*!

SERVES 4–6

For the eel
160g (5¾oz) eel
2 tbsp vegetable oil
1 onion, finely chopped
1 carrot, finely chopped
1 leek, finely chopped
3 sprigs of thyme
2 garlic cloves, peeled and finely chopped

160g (5¾oz) braised ham hock meat, chopped
salt and black freshly ground pepper
1 tbsp sherry vinegar
2 tsp English mustard powder
small bunch of flat leaf parsley
grated zest of **1** lemon
120ml (4fl oz) apple juice
1 Granny Smith apple, cut into 10 balls with a melon baller and quickly cooked

1 Heat the oil in a pan over a low heat. Add the onion, carrot, leek, thyme and garlic and cook until soft. Add enough water so that the eel will be completely submerged once added, then bring to a simmer (do not let it boil). Add the eel to the liquid and bring back to a simmer, then cook for 30 minutes or until the eel gives when gently pressed. When cooked remove the eel (reserve the liquid). Pin-bone and dice the eel meat, and put into a bowl.

2 In a medium-sized bowl, season the ham hock with salt, pepper, sherry vinegar, mustard and parsley.

3 Season the eel with salt, pepper and the lemon zest.

4 Mix the apple juice with the eel liquid and pour some into both eel and ham hock bowls and mix well.

5 Layer 20g (³⁄₄oz) of the ham hock meat in the bottom of a normal-sized cake tin (20cm/8in in diameter) or loaf tin and add 1 tablespoon of the apple juice and eel liquid mixture.

6 Mix 40g (1½ oz) of the eel meat with 10 Granny Smith apple balls and layer this mixture on top of the ham. Pour over 1 tablespoon more of the apple juice and eel cooking liquid.

7 Build up the layers until all the meat is used, finishing with a layer of ham hock. Press the layers down into the cake tin. Add enough of the remaining apple juice and eel liquid mixture to cover. Chill for 4 hours in the refrigerator before serving. Serve in slices with some dressed watercress leaves.

Basil Bavarois
Daniel Clifford | Midsummer House

A clever twist on Bavarian crème, the vibrant green of the basil bavarois alongside the radiant strawberries makes this the ideal dessert to end any outdoor dining experience

SERVES 4

3 gelatine leaves, soaked
100ml (3½fl oz) whipping cream,
  softly whipped
250g (9oz) first-grade
  strawberries
1kg (2lb 4oz) clotted cream
4 vanilla pods, split lengthways

For the basil purée
2 bunches of basil (remove
  stalks and reserve for the
  strawberry marinade), blanched
200ml (⅓ pint) water
200g (7oz) granulated sugar

For the crème anglaise
52g (1¾oz) egg yolk
  (from about 3 eggs)
100g (3½oz) caster sugar
250ml (9fl oz) milk
125ml (4fl oz) double cream
1 vanilla pod, deseeded

1   First, purée all the ingredients for the basil purée, then pass the mixture through a sieve and chill.

2   Next make the crème anglaise. Whisk together the egg yolk and sugar in a large bowl. Bring the milk, cream and vanilla pod to the boil, then pour half of the mixture over the egg and sugar, whisking all the time. Bring the rest of the milk, cream and vanilla mixture back to the boil and pour this into the egg and sugar mixture. Transfer everything back to the pan and heat to 85°C (185°F), stirring continuously. Strain into a bowl set over ice. Leave to cool, then chill in the refrigerator until ready to use.

3   Warm 100ml (3½fl oz) of the créme anglaise and stir in the gelatine leaves. Add 200g (7oz) basil purée and leave to set, then beat to a smooth purée. Lightly fold the whipped cream into the mixture. Pipe or mould the mixture into the desired shape and leave to set for 2–3 hours. Serve with fresh strawberries and vanilla clotted cream (*see* below).

For the vanilla clotted cream
1   Put half of the clotted cream in a pan and heat it gently so that it melts. Add the vanilla pods to the melting cream.

2   Put the remaining clotted cream in a bowl and loosely beat, then fold in the melted cream.

3   Leave to set in the refrigerator for 12 hours.

PUB-FOOD

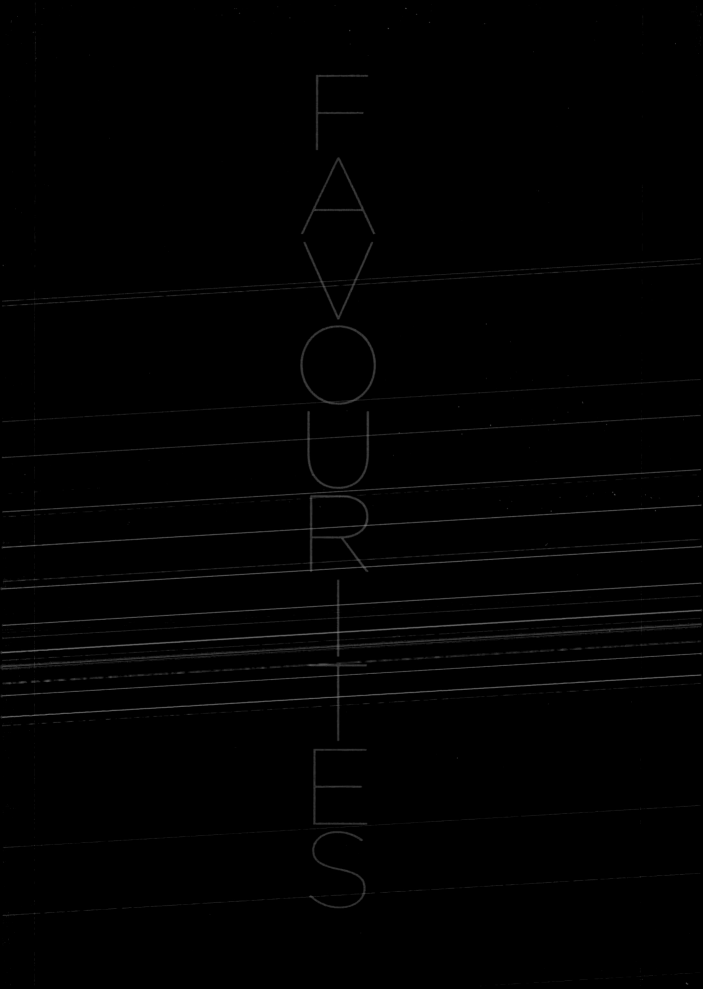

Cow Pie
Jesse Dunford Wood | The Mall Tavern

Although Desperate Dan has been eating this since *The Dandy* launched in 1937, it only featured in *GQ* for the first time in 2012. According to head chef Jesse Dunford Wood, this should be served with a pint of bitter and, of course, a bone protruding from the crust.

SERVES 5

100g (3½oz) peeled baby onions
100g (3½oz) sliced onions
100g (3½oz) sliced mushrooms
10g (¼oz) chopped fresh thyme
50g (1¾oz) butter
salt and freshly ground black pepper
75g (2½oz) plain flour
600ml (1 pint) ale
500g (1lb 2oz) chicken stock (the ale/stock ratio can be altered to your preference)
Dijon mustard
1kg (2lb 4oz) stewing beef, diced
puff pastry
beaten egg yolk

For the bone marrow pie raiser
200g (7oz) marrow bones
15g (½oz) flat leaf parsley, leaves picked and finely chopped
15g (½oz) shallots, finely chopped
1 tsp Dijon mustard
40g (1½oz) breadcrumbs
salt and freshly ground black pepper

Chef's Tip
If the Cow Pie isn't quite beefy enough for you, try swapping the puff pastry for a suet pudding topping.

1 Stew the onions (sliced and baby) and mushrooms together with the chopped thyme in butter, seasoning well, until soft.

2 Add the flour, then pour in the ale and chicken stock. Bring this mixture to the boil and season again with salt, pepper and a bit of Dijon, to taste.

3 Add the beef and cook out like a good old-fashioned casserole for 3 hours at 150°C/fan 130°C/300°F/gas mark 2, or on a low setting.

4 When the beef is tender (we call it 'fork-friendly'), leave it to cool down. Once it is cool, you can top the pie with puff pastry, brush it with egg yolk and, if you can find one, stuff a bone marrow pie raiser (*see* below) in the middle for authenticity, just like at The Mall Tavern.

For the bone marrow pie raiser

1 Soak the marrow bones in water overnight.

2 Next day, drain the marrow bones. Chop the extracted marrow, then mix it with the other bone marrow ingredients and set aside.

3 Boil the bones in water for 1 hour, then drain and allow them to cool. Scrape off the excess gristle from the bones so that the bones are perfectly clean. Stuff the marrow mix back into the bone and use them as pie raisers – use one bone per pie.

Pork Chop with Gherkins
Pierre Koffmann | Koffmann's

One of the world's greatest chefs, Pierre Koffmann was once at the forefront of the nouvelle cuisine movement, but his heart has always belonged to traditional French gastronomy or, as he calls it, cuisine de terroir (food of the earth). This pan-roasted recipe sums up the brilliance and the simplicity of his cooking.

SERVES 4

50g (1¾oz) duck fat
4 pork rib chops
75g (2½oz) onions, finely sliced
1 sprig of thyme
3 garlic cloves, finely sliced
salt and freshly ground black pepper
pickled gherkins, to serve

1 Heat the duck fat in a frying pan, put in the chops and cook for 4 minutes on each side. Transfer the chops to a dish and keep in a warm place.

2 Tip out half of the fat from the pan, then add the onions to the pan and cook until they are soft. Add the thyme, garlic and seasoning, cover and cook for about 8 minutes until soft.

3 Place the chops on the vegetables and heat through for 3 minutes. Check the seasoning, stir in the gherkins and serve with broccoli and pan-roasted potatoes.

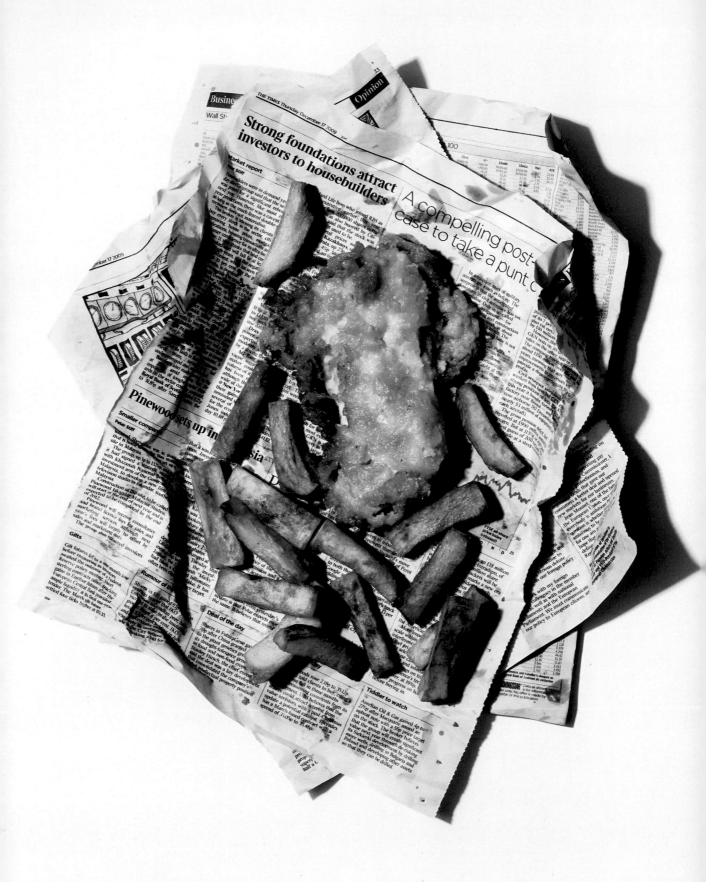

Beer and Vodka Battered Fish 'n' Triple-Cooked Chips

Heston Blumenthal | The Hinds Head

'I became obsessed with chips around 1992, before I had even opened the Fat Duck,' Blumenthal told *GQ*. 'I wanted chips with a glass-like crust and a soft, fluffy centre.' Triple-cooked chips were the result of tinkering with technique, and a strong vision of what he was searching for from an ingredient. This is the ubiquitously imitated recipe for triple-cooked chips, created by Heston in 1993.

SERVES 4

200g (7oz) plain flour
200g (7oz) white rice flour, plus extra for dusting
1 tsp baking powder
1 tbsp honey
300ml (½ pint) vodka
300ml (½ pint) lager
2–3 litres (3½–5¼ pints) groundnut oil, for frying
4 large turbot fillets, 2–3cm (¾–1¼in) thick (ideally, get 1 whole turbot weighing 2.5kg/5lb 8oz and either fillet it yourself, or get the fishmonger to do it)
salt and freshly ground black pepper

For the chips
1.2kg (2lb 12oz) Arran Victory or Maris Piper potatoes, peeled
table salt and sea salt
2–3 litres (3½–5¼ pints) groundnut oil

Chef's Tip
For the authentic chip shop experience, take some juice from a jar of pickled onions (or some white wine vinegar) and place it into an atomiser and squirt it over the fish 'n' chips.

1 Tip the flours and baking powder into a bowl. Put the honey and vodka into a jug, stir and add to the flour. Open the can of lager, measure out the quantity needed and immediately stir it into the batter until just combined. It doesn't matter if the batter is a little lumpy. Transfer the batter to a jug, then pour it into a soda syphon. Charge the syphon with three CO_2 charges and put it in the refrigerator for a minimum of 30 minutes.

2 Put enough groundnut oil into a large pan or casserole to cover the fish. Heat it to 220°C (425°F). Rinse the turbot fillets and dry them with kitchen paper. Season well, then dust with rice flour. Shake off any excess flour.

3 Shake the syphon vigorously, then squirt just enough batter to cover 1 fillet into a medium-sized bowl. Dip the fillet into the foamy batter. When it is completely coated, lower the fillet into the hot oil. Repeat with the other fillets. As the fish fry, drizzle a little extra batter over them to give a lovely crusty exterior. When they are a light golden brown, turn them over and drizzle more batter on top, then let them cook for another minute or so, until they are a deeper golden brown, then remove from the oil. Use a digital thermometer in the thickest part of each fillet to check it is cooked – at 40°C (104°F) the fillet should be set aside so the residual heat will cook it to a temperature of 45°C (113°F). Serve with chips (*see* below).

For the chips

1 Cut the peeled potatoes into chips about 1.5cm (⁵⁄₈in) thick. Put them in a bowl and place it under cold running water for 2–3 minutes, then drain.

2 Bring a large pan of salted water to the boil, add the chips, bring back to the boil and simmer gently until they have almost broken up (the fissures that form as the potato breaks up trap the fat, creating a crunchy crust). Carefully transfer to a wire rack using a slotted spoon. Leave to cool, then refrigerate until cold.

3 Pour enough oil to cover the chips into a deep-fat fryer and heat to 130°C (266°F). Plunge in the chips and cook until slighly coloured, with a dry appearance. Remove, drain off excess fat, then transfer to a wire rack. Once cool, refrigerate until cold.

4 Reheat the oil to 190°C (375°F). Plunge in the chips and cook until golden brown. Drain, season well with a mixture of table and sea salt, then pile them next to the fish.

Lasagne
Marco Torri | Bar Trattoria Semplice

The key to this dish is getting the very best ingredients, especially the beef. If you can, get your butcher to mince some decent steak and start from there. The rest is easy and we guarantee you'll make this again and again.

SERVES 4

For the béchamel
60g (2¼oz) butter
60g (2¼oz) plain flour
1 litre (1¾ pints) milk, warmed

For the bolognese
100g (3½oz) chopped onions
100g (3½oz) chopped celery
100g (3½oz) chopped carrots
olive oil
500g (1lb 2oz) top-quality
  minced beef
pinch of salt
150ml (¼ pint) red wine
2 x 400g (14oz) cans plum
  tomatoes
dried lasagne sheets
  (De Cecco or Barilla)
Parmesan cheese, grated

For the béchamel (white sauce)
1 Heat the butter in a pan, then add the flour and cook for 10 minutes until the mixture has a honeycomb consistency. Slowly add the warm milk to the roux in stages, stirring continually until the mixture has a sauce-like consistency.

For the bolognese
1 Sweat the chopped vegetables in olive oil, then add the mince and a pinch of salt. When all the liquid from the mince has evaporated, add the red wine and, when this has evaporated, add the canned plum tomatoes. Cook gently for 2 hours over a very low heat.

2 Preheat the oven to 180°C/fan 160°C/350°F/gas mark 4. Mix the bolognese with the béchamel. Check the seasoning.

3 In a large ovenproof dish, add a couple of ladles of sauce. Lay a sheet of pasta on top. Add more sauce on the top of the pasta and spread with Parmesan. Continue to layer the pasta, sauce and cheese until the dish is full, then bake for 35–40 minutes.

Prawns in Kerala Curry
Vivek Singh | Cinnamon Club

The state of Kerala on the south-west coast of India is well-known for the richness of its cuisine, and this curry recipe from Vivek Singh showcases all that is good about the area. From the use of king prawns to the rich spicy tomato sauce, this is a modern take on a regional classic.

SERVES 4–6

4 tbsp vegetable or corn oil
½ **tsp** black peppercorns
1 tsp mustard seeds
½ **tsp** fenugreek seeds
10 fresh curry leaves
2 red onions, chopped
½ **tsp** ground turmeric
1 tsp ground coriander
2 tsp mild red chilli powder
2 tomatoes, finely chopped
1 tsp salt
20 king prawns, peeled and deveined
4 kokum berries (or **2 tbsp** tamarind paste)
150ml (¼ pint) seafood stock (or fish stock)
200ml (⅓ pint) coconut milk

1 Heat the oil in a pan, add the peppercorns and the mustard and fenugreek seeds, followed by the curry leaves and onions. Sauté until golden brown.

2 Add the ground spices, tomatoes and salt and cook the mixture until the tomatoes have disintegrated.

3 Add the prawns and toss well for 3–5 minutes.

4 Stir in the kokum berries and stock and simmer for 2–3 minutes.

5 Now stir in the coconut milk and simmer for 3–5 minutes until the sauce has a creamy consistency. Serve immediately with steamed rice.

Salt and Pepper Squid
Jason Atherton | Pollen Street Social

Once you start tucking into Jason Atherton's salt and pepper squid, you'll find it almost impossible to stop. The tempura batter makes each nugget light and crispy, which provides a lovely contrast to the baby squid.

SERVES 4 as a starter

400g (14oz) baby squid, cleaned
½ a 100g (3½oz) packet
  tempura batter mix
5 heaped tbsp plain flour
1 tsp fine sea salt
1 tsp freshly ground black pepper
groundnut oil, for deep-frying
coarse sea salt
1 green chilli, finely sliced
1 red chilli, finely sliced
4 lime wedges, to serve

1 Pull the tentacles away from the squid and slice the body pouches into rings. Pat dry with kitchen paper.

2 Make up the tempura batter according to the packet instructions and set aside. Put the flour into a bowl and season with salt and pepper.

3 Heat the groundnut oil to 180°C (350°F) in a deep-fat fryer or heavy-based pan. Dip the squid into the seasoned flour, then shake off any excess flour. Draw the squid through the tempura batter and deep-fry in small batches for 1–1½ minutes until lightly golden and crisp. Drain on kitchen paper.

4 Sprinkle the deep-fried rings and tentacles with a little coarse sea salt and scatter over the sliced chillies. Serve immediately, with the lime wedges.

Chef's Tip
To make this dish extra special, add a little seared otoro tuna. Simply sear the fish, then arrange the squid salad on top. This combination of crispy squid and top-grade tuna belly will blow your guests away.

Scotch Eggs
Heston Blumenthal | The Hinds Head

Across the road from his three-Michelin starred restaurant The Fat Duck, sits Heston Blumenthal's pub, The Hinds Head. On the menu you'll find a selection of classic British dishes, but the Scotch egg is a real work of genius. 'I use quail eggs, which means they are smaller than normal,' Blumenthal said. 'But that combination of warm yolk, well-seasoned sausage meat and a crispy coating is irresistible.' Runny yolk Scotch eggs now appear all over the UK, but this is the Heston original.

MAKES 12

12 quail eggs
480g (1lb 1oz) best-quality pork sausagemeat
salt and freshly ground black pepper
cayenne pepper
plain flour
3 eggs, beaten
150g (5½oz) white homemade breadcrumbs, dried out in a low oven, or panko breadcrumbs
oil, for deep-frying

1 Put a pan of water on to boil, then prick the tops of the quail eggs with a cocktail stick. Have a container of iced water ready, then cook the eggs for 2 minutes and 15 seconds exactly. As soon as your timer goes off, transfer the eggs from the boiling water to the ice bath.

2 Season the sausagemeat with salt, black pepper and a pinch of cayenne pepper, then check the seasoning by frying a small amount of seasoned sausagemeat (or microwaving it for 20–30 seconds) and tasting. The meat will need to be well seasoned. Adjust the seasoning as necessary.

3 Peel the shells from the eggs, then wrap each egg in 40g (1½oz) sausagemeat. To do this, roll the meat into a ball, then flatten it into a shape big enough to go around the egg. Wrap it around the egg and press the edges together to seal, taking care not to squash the egg inside.

4 Prepare three bowls: one with plain flour, one with the beaten eggs and one with breadcrumbs. (If using panko breadcrumbs, break them up between the fingers to make it easier to coat the sausagemeat.) Roll the meat-covered eggs in the flour, tap to remove any excess flour, then roll them in the beaten egg and, finally, the breadcrumbs. Put the coated eggs in the freezer for 5 minutes to harden the coating, then dip each coated egg again in the beaten egg and breadcrumbs.

5 Heat the oil in a deep-fat fryer or heavy-based pan, then deep-fry the coated eggs for 2–3 minutes until golden brown. Finish in a hot oven at 200°C/fan 180°C/400°F/gas mark 6 for 2–3 minutes.

Sausage Roll
Claude Bosi | The Fox and Grapes

Inspired by his daughter's love of the sausage roll, Claude Bosi decided that if he was going to make one, it would be using only the very best ingredients. When you make this yourself, the results will speak for themselves.

MAKES 12

For the 'brown sauce' dressing
440ml (15½fl oz) truffle jus, reduced over high heat to a glaze (it should coat the back of a spoon)
150ml (5½fl oz) vegetable oil
1 tbsp sherry vinegar

For the sausage roll
600g (1lb 5oz) pork (shoulder and neck)
120g (4¼oz) raw foie gras
salt and either black pepper or four-spice blend
50g (1¾oz) black Périgord truffle or wild mushroom duxelles
500g (1lb 2oz) puff pastry
beaten organic egg yolk, to glaze

Chef's Tip
Bosi has one rule: no ketchup. 'Try my brown sauce truffle dressing instead. It works perfectly with the sausage roll.'

For the 'brown sauce' dressing
1 Blend together the ingredients for the dressing for 3 minutes, then leave the mixture to rest at room temperature.

For the sausage roll
1 Mince the pork and foie gras together, adding a pinch of salt and either four-spice blend or black pepper.

2 Chop the truffle or duxelles and add to the pork. Mix well, then divide the mixture into 12 balls of 80g (3oz).

3 Roll out the puff pastry into 2 sheets, each with a thickness of 5mm (¼in). From these, cut 12 oblongs that are each 23 x 12cm (9 x 5in). Rest the pastry in the refrigerator for 20 minutes. Preheat the oven to 180°C/fan 160°C/350°F/gas mark 4.

4 Take the pastry sheets and glaze each of them along the edges with beaten egg yolk. Arrange one piece of meat at one end of a pastry sheet. Fold the pastry over the meat, then press around the edges to ensure it is all sealed and glazed. Repeat with the remaining meat and pastry. Place the sausage rolls on a baking sheet and cook on the top shelf of the oven for 12 minutes or until golden brown. Serve with a dollop of 'brown sauce' and a generous winter leaf salad.

Lamb Tagine
Jeff Galvin | Galvin La Chapelle

Although usually associated with classic French cooking, this Moroccan-inspired lamb dish, by one half of the hugely talented and successful Galvin brothers, benefits from seriously slow cooking, allowing the meat to melt off the bone and into the rich and fragrant gravy.

SERVES 4

4 x 300g (10½oz) lamb
 shoulder shanks
oil
2 large carrots, diced
2 celery sticks, cut into 4cm
 (1½in) lengths
1 leek, roughly chopped
1 large onion, quartered
3 garlic cloves
1 tsp ground cinnamon
1 small piece of fresh root ginger
½ tsp whole cumin
¼ cinnamon stick
1 tsp allspice berries
1 tsp cardamoms
1 tsp coriander seeds
1 tsp four-spice blend
250ml (9fl oz) white wine
4 litres (7 pints) brown lamb stock
rose harissa, to taste
100g (3½oz) steamed couscous,
 mixed with soaked raisins,
 chopped pepper, diced olives
 and finished with olive oil and
 roughly 2 tsp chopped fresh
 mint and coriander
4 tbsp wilted spinach
4 soft-boiled quail eggs
1 salt-preserved lemon,
 quartered
4 bastilla (spiced date
 chutney rolled in pate à bric
 or filo pastry) and baked
 until golden
8 dessertspoons aubergine
 caviar
extra virgin olive oil

1 Preheat the oven to 110°C/fan 90°C/225°F/ gas mark ¼. Brown the lamb in oil in a casserole dish or heavy-based ovenproof saucepan, then remove the lamb and set aside. Now brown the vegetables and garlic in the same pan.

2 Add the spices and cook gently to lightly toast them, being careful not to burn them.

3 Add the lamb, wine and stock, bring to the boil, skim and cover with a lid. Transfer the casserole to the oven and cook for 2½ hours. Remove from the oven and allow the lamb to cool in the cooking liquor. (When braising meat, always allow it to cool in the cooking liquor. This will make the meat much more moist.)

4 Remove the lamb carefully and wrap it in foil to keep warm. Set aside. Pass the cooking liquor through a fine sieve or muslin cloth. Now reduce the liquid by half and finish the sauce by adding a little rose harissa to taste.

5 Spoon equal amounts of the couscous mixture onto the centre of each plate. Place a quarter of the wilted spinach onto each plate and top each pile with a quail egg. Arrange the salted lemon on each plate, with a baked bastilla next to it. Spoon 2 quenelles of aubergine caviar onto each plate. Now arrange a hot lamb shoulder on top of the couscous, drizzle extra virgin oil on top, then spoon lamb jus around. Serve with the rose harissa sauce.

French Onion Soup

Raymond Blanc |
Le Manoir aux Quat'Saisons

Unsurprisingly, for legendary chef Raymond Blanc, this humble soup is all about the onions. 'For this dish to really work, you want a high sugar content and high acidity,' he said. 'For me, the best onions are Pink Roscoff.' You have been told.

SERVES 4

4 tbsp unsalted butter, diced
4 pink Roscoff or Spanish onions, finely sliced
10 pinches of salt
2 pinches of freshly ground black pepper
1 tbsp plain flour
200ml (⅓ pint) dry white wine, boiled for 30 seconds to burn off the alcohol
1.4 litres (2½ pints) boiling water
1 tsp sugar
½ baguette, cut into 12 thick slices
150g (5½oz) Gruyère cheese, grated

1   Preheat the oven to 200°C/fan 180°C/400°F/gas mark 6. Over a high heat, melt the butter in a pan, add the onions and soften for 5 minutes. Add the salt and pepper. Continue cooking for 20–30 minutes for a caramel colour.

2   Meanwhile, sprinkle the flour on a baking sheet and cook in the oven for 10 minutes until it turns pale brown.

3   Put the flour into the pan with the onions. Stir in the wine and one-third of the boiling water, whisk and add the remaining boiling water. Boil, skim, then reduce the heat and simmer for 15 minutes. Season to taste, adding sugar if required. Preheat the grill on a high setting.

4   Place the baguette slices on a grill pan and sprinkle two-thirds of the Gruyère over them. Melt the cheese under the hot grill for 3–4 minutes until it browns. Serve the soup with the croutons and the rest of the Gruyère.

ROCK 'N' ROLL

ROASTS

Roast Molasses Pigeon with Winter Tabbouleh
Stephen Gadd | The Rookery

'The reason I love this dish is because of its freshness in winter,' Stephen Gadd said of his roasted pigeon. With colourful and refreshing tabbouleh, the molasses making the pigeon slightly sweeter, and the richness and depth of flavour of the hazelnuts, you will almost forget it is cold outside.

SERVES 4 as a starter or 2 as a main course

2 pigeons
150ml (¼ pint) pomegranate molasses

For the winter tabbouleh
200g (7oz) bulgur wheat
salt and freshly ground black pepper
½ fennel bulb, finely chopped
½ chicory, finely chopped
100g (3½oz) cauliflower florets
1 pomegranate, deseeded (reserve a few seeds for sprinkling)
small handful of roughly chopped flat leaf parsley
small handful of roughly chopped fresh coriander

For the tabbouleh dressing
1 garlic clove, chopped
lemon juice
100ml (3½fl oz) pomegranate molasses
1 pinch of ground cinnamon
100ml (3½fl oz) olive oil

For the hazelnut sauce
100g (3½oz) hazelnuts, roasted and roughly chopped (reserve a few for sprinkling)
juice of ½ and grated rind of **1** orange
small bunch of fresh mint, chopped
50ml (2fl oz) good-quality vinegar
75ml (2½fl oz) olive oil

1 Put the pigeons in the pomegranate molasses, cover with clingfilm and place in the refrigerator for an hour to marinate.

2 For the tabbouleh, place the bulgur wheat in a bowl and just cover with warm water. Add a good pinch of salt, cover with clingfilm and leave for 8 minutes. Fork through the bulgur wheat and season. It should still have a little bite to it. Add the chopped vegetables, pomegranate seeds and chopped herbs.

3 For the dressing, put the garlic in a bowl and add lemon juice to taste. Add the pomegranate molasses, a good pinch of ground cinnamon and the olive oil. Mix well.

4 For the hazelnut sauce, combine the hazelnuts, the orange rind and juice and the chopped mint in a bowl or jug, then stir in the vinegar and oil.

5 Preheat the oven to 200°C/fan 180°C/400°F/gas mark 6. Dress the tabbouleh with the dressing and set aside (not in the refrigerator).

6 Remove the pigeons from the marinade, place on a baking tray and roast for 6 minutes. Reduce the oven temperature to 180°C/fan 160°C/350°F/ gas mark 4 and cook for a further 4 minutes for medium-rare, 6 minutes for medium or 10 minutes for medium/well done. Take the pigeons out of the oven and rest them for 8 minutes before carving.

7 Taste the tabbouleh – it shouldn't be refrigerator cold. Place the tabbouleh on plates, then position the carved pigeon on top with some hazelnuts. Finish with the sauce and a sprinkling of pomegranate seeds.

Roast Chicken, Maple Vegetables and Roasting Juices
Paul Ainsworth | Number 6 Restaurant

Rather than roasting a whole chicken, this recipe from Paul Ainsworth uses pieces of chicken that are poached first, then finished in the pan.

SERVES 4

4 chicken legs, boned (ask the butcher for the bones and the carcass, too)
4 chicken breasts, French trimmed
100ml (3½fl oz) olive oil, plus extra for frying
small handful of thyme flowers
rock salt and freshly ground black pepper
3 carrots, peeled
500ml (18fl oz) chicken stock
30g (1oz) fresh thyme
30g (1oz) fresh rosemary
3 bay leaves
3 red onions
3 small white onions
100g (3½oz) butter, chilled, plus extra to thicken the sauce
50ml (2fl oz) maple syrup
lemon juice (optional)

Chef's tip
For a more gamey flavour, this dish works just as well with guinea fowl.

1 First marinate the chicken legs and breasts in the olive oil mixed with the thyme flowers, salt and pepper for 2 hours.

2 Place a pan of water on the stove and bring the temperature up to about 85°C/185°F. Wrap the marinated chicken breasts individually in clingfilm as tightly as possible so they don't let in any water. Do the same with the legs and tie knots at both ends of the clingfilm. Poach the legs in the water for 45 minutes and the breasts for 10 minutes, them remove and leave to cool in the clingfilm.

3 Put the carrots in a pan and cover with some of the chicken stock, add a pinch of thyme leaves, a pinch of rosemary leaves and 1 bay leaf, then cook until soft. Do the same with the onions, keeping the red and white onions in separate pans. Cook until you can put a knife through the middle easily. Leave the vegetables to cool in the liquor. Once cool, take them out, drain off the liquor into a pan and reduce by half.

4 Preheat the oven to 190°C/fan 170°C/375°F/gas mark 5. Take the bones and carcass from the butcher and roast them in the oven so they take on a golden colour and release their roast flavour. Place the bones in the reduced liquid and simmer gently for 10 minutes, then pull off the heat.

5 Cut the carrots into batons and the onions into thirds. Drain them on kitchen paper to keep them slightly dry. Add any juices from the vegetables to the chicken bones in the pan. Remove the chicken from the clingfilm and pat dry. Place 2 frying pans on the stove with a little olive oil and half the butter in each and heat gently. When foaming, put the legs and breasts in one pan and colour them all over to form a crispy skin. Add the vegetables to the other pan and colour also, adding a sprig of thyme and rosemary and some seasoning.

6 Drain off excess butter from the vegetables and add the maple syrup. This will caramelize the onions and carrots. When glazed, place them on a tray. Do the same with the chicken.

7 Pass off the reduced stock in a sieve set over a bowl, pushing down as hard as you can with a ladle to extract every bit of chicken flavour from the bones. Warm up the liquid and whisk in a little cold butter just to thicken the sauce. Check for seasoning and maybe add a squeeze of lemon juice. Place a leg and breast on each plate with the vegetables. Pour over your roast chicken sauce and serve with Cornish new potatoes.

Roast Shropshire Partridge
Claude Bosi | Hibiscus

With its lean and subtle gamey flavour, roast partridge is at its best in the autumn months and makes a delicious and less fussy alternative to roasting a whole chicken. This recipe requires roasting and simmering in chicken stock to keep the flesh tender and moist.

SERVES 4

2 oven-ready partridges
200g (7oz) butter, plus extra for cooking the vegetables
150g (5oz) smoked butter
3 litres (6 pints 7fl oz) chicken stock
4 tbsp olive oil
½ pumpkin, sliced into quarters (skin left on)
Fleur de sel or sea salt
10g (½oz) chopped parsley
2 carrots, peeled and chopped into 2cm (¾in) batons
2 parsley roots, peeled and cut into triangles
seeds from **1** pomegranate, to garnish

For the caper and raisin sauce
100g (3½oz) raisins
100g (3½oz) capers
chicken stock
200g (7oz) salted butter

1   Preheat the oven to 180°C/fan 160°C/350°F/gas mark 4. Remove the legs from the partridges and set the crowns aside.

2   Set the legs in a deep roasting pan with 200g (7oz) butter and the smoked butter, then confit the legs in the oven for about 20 minutes. Remove the pan from the oven, pour over the chicken stock and simmer on the hob, turning the legs regularly, for approximately 1 hour or until soft. Once cooked, remove the legs from the pan and leave to cool.

3   Reheat the oven to 180°C/fan 160°C/350°F/gas mark 4. Heat 2 tablespoons of oil in a large flameproof pan. Add the partridge crowns and cook for 4 minutes on each side, then roast in the oven for 3 minutes. Remove from the oven and leave to rest for 5 minutes.

4   Put the pumpkin in a roasting pan with a little butter, salt and chopped parsley, and roast in the oven, turning occasionally, for 10–15 minutes or until soft.

5   Melt a little butter in a small roasting pan over a medium heat and add the carrots and parsley root. Transfer the pan to the oven and roast for 10–15 minutes or until soft.

6   Finish the partridge *á la minute*. Fillet the breasts fom the crowns. Trim the end bones off the legs. Heat the remaining 2 tablespoons of oil in a pan over a high heat. Add the breasts and legs, crisp the skin and heat through. To serve, arrange the roasted vegetables on one side of warm serving plates and place a partridge in the centre. Pour over the caper and raisin sauce (*see* below) and garnish with pomegranate seeds.

For the caper and raisin sauce
1   Place the raisins and capers in a pan. Add enough chicken stock to cover and bring to the boil to rehydrate the raisins. Pour into a blender and blitz with butter until smooth. Pass the sauce through a sieve before serving.

Haunch of Wild Boar with Pineapple, Cavolo Nero and Blueberry and Gin Sauce
Rasheed Shahin | The Club Bar & Dining

Although this dish originally featured in *GQ* as an alternative Christmas lunch, it really makes a great Sunday roast alternative at any time of the year. Plus, because wild pork contains much less fat than domestic-production pork it is a tasty and healthy alternative. Furthermore, haunch is a cut that contains very little fat, so this is as lean as a good roast gets.

SERVES 6-8

1 haunch of wild boar, about 2.5-3kg (5lb 8oz-6lb 8oz)
juice from 3 lemons
salt and pepper
1 bunch of fresh rosemary
2-3 star anise
250ml (9fl oz) gin
1kg (2lb 4oz) mirepoix (a mixture of chopped carrots, leeks and white onions)
1 bunch of fresh thyme
1 litre (1¾ pints) water
2 pineapples, peeled, cored and sliced into rings
100g (3½oz) sugar
1 punnet of blueberries
50g (1¾oz) butter
1kg (2lb 4oz) cavolo nero, shredded
pinch of ground nutmeg

1 The haunch is the leg of the boar and contains very little fat. The meat should be soaked in cold water and lemon juice overnight to loosen it up – the boar is a wild animal and its flesh can be quite tough.

2 Preheat the oven to 160°C/fan 140°C/325°F/gas mark 3. Place the haunch on a large board and season well with salt and pepper. Add sprigs of rosemary, the star anise and a splash of gin. Bind the haunch with kitchen string to keep its shape, then place it on a rack over an oven tray (to catch the fat and the juices during cooking).

3 At the bottom of the oven tray arrange the *mirepoix*, plus the thyme and more rosemary. Cover the vegetables with the water – this will give you the base for the sauce. Place the tray in the oven with the meat on the rack above and cook for 1 hour 45 minutes.

4 Place the pineapple rings in a large pan with the sugar, the blueberries (reserve a good handful for garnishing) and a little water. Cook over a medium heat for 15 minutes until the pineapple is soft. Remove from the heat and set aside.

5 Place the butter in another large pan and add the cavolo nero and nutmeg. Season with salt and pepper. Cook for 4 minutes, then remove from the heat.

6 To present the dish, transfer the cavolo nero to a large serving tray and arrange the pineapple rings around the outside. Take the haunch out of the oven, slice it and place the slices on top of the cavolo nero.

7 For the sauce, strain the liquid from the roasting pan and set it aside. Deglaze the pan with the rest of the gin and reduce by half. Return the reserved liquid to the pan and reduce again. Strain the sauce into a clean pan, add the blueberries and heat for a few minutes, then serve.

Chef's Tip
To get your hands on some good-quality wild boar, try the Suffolk-based Wild Meat Company (www.wildmeat.co.uk) or alternatively, Just Wild Boar (www.thinc.co.uk/JWB/index.htm).

Roast Breast of Goose with Mulled Wine Sauce

Lawrence Keogh | Roast

'Goose is intensely flavoured, full bodied and delicious in that wonderfully gamey way,' says Lawrence Keogh from the aptly named restaurant, Roast. And because almost all the geese in the UK are free-range, you will also be doing your bit for ethical eating.

SERVES 2

For the mulled wine sauce
75ml (2½fl oz) red wine vinegar
150g (5½oz) sugar
300ml (½ pint) red wine
¼ cinnamon stick
5 cloves

For the goose
1 large goose breast, trimmed of any sinew
salt and freshly ground black pepper

To garnish
1 clementine or satsuma, segmented and sliced
50g (1¾oz) Brussels sprouts, cooked and refreshed
watercress
50g (1¾oz) cranberries
½ pomegranate, deseeded

1 Place the vinegar, sugar, wine, cinnamon and cloves in a pan and reduce the liquid for 15 minutes or until there is 300ml (½ pint) remaining. Pour this into a jar and reserve. Preheat the oven to 200°C/fan 180°C/400°F/gas mark 6.

2 Season the goose breast and place it skin-side down in a hot flameproof pan, then roast it in the oven for 12 minutes. Rest the breast for 10 minutes.

3 Reheat the sauce. Slice the goose breast and assemble the slices on two plates. Sprinkle the garnishes around the outside of the slices, then gently spoon over the mulled wine sauce. Serve with some boiled potatoes rolled in parsley, chives and butter.

Chef's Tip
Goose can be fatty, but the beauty of that is you can use all that rendered fat to make the most delicious roast potatoes.

Roast Lamb with Pomegranate
Simon Schama

The key to this slow-roasted lamb is to make a marinade using pomegranate molasses. This give the meat a sweet tenderness and a bold aroma that will leave your guests gobsmacked. Serve it with a winter salad of chicory and shredded spiced cabbage.

SERVES 4

1 bone-in leg of lamb (around 2kg/4lb 8oz)
300ml (½ pint) pomegranate molasses diluted with 100ml (3½fl oz) water
3 garlic cloves, crushed
2 tbsp light olive oil
1 dried red chilli, crumbled
1 tbsp sumac
salt and freshly ground black pepper

1 After breakfast, strip away all the fat and silky membranes from the lamb, then score the meat all over the joint. Mix the pomegranage molasses and water mixture with the garlic, olive oil, chilli and sumac. Set the lamb joint in a glass bowl, pour over the marinade and marinate for 3–4 hours.

2 At 11 o'clock, turn over the lamb. At around 3 o'clock, preheat the oven to 210°C/fan 190°C/410°F/gas mark 6½. Set the joint in a deep roasting pan, keeping the bits of marinade that are clinging to it. Reduce the oven temperature to 110°C/fan 90°C/225°F/gas mark ¼ and roast the lamb very gently for 3½ hours, turning once. The flesh should be spoon-soft without falling off the bone. Rest the roast lamb for 20 minutes or so before serving.

3 While the lamb is resting, deglaze the remaining marinade with a few tablespoons of water, scooping up the tasty bits in the roasting pan. Adjust the seasoning if necessary. Strain the liquid and you'll end with a fine, rich, dark sauce to serve with the lamb. There are few things I like less than cold roast lamb, but this dish is an exception. The pomegranate continues to perfume the meat even when cold. This works brilliantly with a winter salad of chicory and shredded spiced cabbage.

Roast Chicken with New-season Garlic
Mark Hix | Hix Oyster and Chop House

This simple recipe for roast chicken is, as Mark Hix maintains, all about being respectful to the quality of the ingredients being used. That's why you should get the best free-range bird you can. Take our word for it – you will notice the difference.

SERVES 4-6

1 free-range chicken, about
  1.5kg (3lb 5oz)
a few sprigs of thyme and
  rosemary
a few generous knobs of butter
100g (3½oz) chicken livers
chopped fresh parsley, to garnish

For the stuffing
60g (2¼oz) butter
1 medium onion, finely chopped
100g (3½oz) chicken livers,
  chopped
2 tsp fresh thyme leaves
sea salt and freshly ground
  black pepper
80-100g (3-3½oz) fresh white
  breadcrumbs
2 tbsp chopped fresh parsley

For the garlic sauce
4 heads of new-season garlic
small bunch of flat leaf parsley
½ tbsp Dijon mustard
2-3 tbsp warm duck fat (or
  chicken juices)
60-70g (2¼-2½oz) fresh white
  breadcrumbs
splash of milk
sea salt and freshly ground black
  pepper

Chef's Tip
Woolley Park Farm
(www.woolleyparkfarm.
co.uk) is a great supplier
of chicken. Their birds
are corn fed and have
an intense, almost
gamey, flavour.

For the stuffing
1 Melt the butter in a pan. Add the onion, livers and thyme, season and cook over a medium heat for 2–3 minutes. Take the pan off the heat and mix in the breadcrumbs and parsley. Season with salt and pepper. Either use this mixture to stuff your bird, or cook it in an ovenproof dish or wrapped in foil for the last 30–40 minutes.

For the chicken
1 Preheat the oven to 200°C/fan 180°C/400°F/gas mark 6. Season the chicken inside and out. Put the herbs into the cavity along with the stuffing, if you are using it to stuff the chicken. Rub butter all over the breast and legs.

2 Put the chicken into a large roasting tin and roast the chicken in the oven, basting regularly. Add the livers to the roasting tin for the last 6 minutes or so. Test the chicken after 1¼ hours by inserting a skewer into the thickest part of the thigh. The juices should run clear.

3 Lift the chicken onto a warmed platter and rest in a warm place for 15 minutes. Sprinkle with chopped parsley and serve with the roasted livers, stuffing and garlic sauce (*see* below).

For the garlic sauce
1 Preheat the oven to 200°C/fan 180°C/400°F/gas mark 6. Wrap the heads of new-season garlic in foil and bake for 1 hour. Unwrap the garlic and set aside until cool enough to handle. Peel away the outer skin and blend with the parsley, mustard, warm duck fat (or chicken juices) and breadcrumbs until smooth. Add enough milk to thicken the sauce and season to taste.

Turducken

Tom Kerridge | The Hand and Flowers

This variation on the traditional 'king of roasts' has been simplified for *GQ* by chef Tom Kerridge from The Hand and Flowers. By using breasts rather than whole birds (turducken refers to turkey, duck and chicken), it is easier to prepare and less fatty, but just as delicious.

SERVES 4

For the stuffing
100g (3½oz) sausagemeat
50g (1¾oz) finely chopped cooked onion
20g (¾oz) chopped chestnuts
20g (¾oz) fresh breadcrumbs
10 fresh sage leaves, chopped
salt and freshly ground black pepper

For the turducken
1 large duck breast
1 chicken breast
1 turkey breast
salt and freshly ground black pepper
rapeseed oil

For the roast potatoes
8 Potato Lovers or Maris Piper potatoes
vegetable oil
salt

For the crushed swede
1 large swede, peeled and diced
butter
salt and cracked black pepper

For the pickled cabbage
500ml (18fl oz) white wine vinegar
½ cinnamon stick
4 star anise
1 tsp fennel seeds
1 tbs coriander seeds
1 tsp white peppercorns
1 tsp Sichuan pepper
300g (10½oz) sugar
1 red cabbage, cut into chunky pieces (including the core)
1 onion, thinly sliced
bunch of chives, chopped
rapeseed oil
salt and freshly ground black pepper

For the stuffing
1 Combine all the stuffing ingredients, mix well and set aside.

For the turducken
1 Remove the skin from the duck and chicken. Place the duck breast between 2 sheets of clingfilm and bash it out to a thickness of about 1.5cm (½in). Do the same with the chicken breast.

2 Lay out the bashed-out chicken breast. Place the stuffing mix in the centre and roll the chicken around it. Now lay out the bashed-out duck breast. Place the chicken in the centre and roll up as before. Cut a slit in the turkey breast (not on the skin side) and fan out the breast so the chicken and duck roll will fit in the hole you've made. Roll the turkey back up and chill for 6–8 hours. Season and drizzle over some rapeseed oil. Heat the oven to 220°C/fan 200°C/425°F/gas mark 7.

3 Place the roll in a roasting pan and cook in the oven for about 25 minutes so that the skin crisps up. Reduce the oven temperature to 120°C/fan 100°C/250°F/gas mark ½ and cook for about 2½ hours. Remove from the oven and rest for 1 hour. Slice and serve with the stuffing and vegetables (*see* below).

4 For the roast potatoes, heat the oven to 200°C/fan 180°C/400°F/gas mark 6. Cut the peeled potatoes into a good size for roasting. Cover them with water in a pan, bring to the boil, season and simmer until they are just soft. Drain and let them steam dry. Pour a layer of oil into a roasting pan and allow it to get hot in the oven. Add the potatoes and roast for about 45 minutes until they are crispy and brown.

5 Blanch the swede until soft, then crush it with a potato masher, adding lots of butter, salt and pepper. Don't stint on the butter – it should taste naughty.

6 To make the cabbage, put the vinegar, spices and sugar into a pan and bring to the boil. Take the pan off the heat and allow the liquor to infuse for 30 minutes, then pass it through a sieve and leave to cool. Place the cabbage in the pickle mix and leave for at least 1 hour, then drain, mix with the onion, sprinkle with chopped chives and drizzle with rapeseed oil. Season to taste.

Whole Stone Bass with Sumac, Orange and Fennel
Chris Golding | Apero

Although this recipe uses stone bass, you could use grouper or turbot, but do try to get your hands on the sumac. Commonly used in Arabic and Lebanese cooking, it has a mildly tangy sweet-and-sour taste that works wonderfully with firm white fish and chicken.

SERVES 2-3

2 large fennel, each cut into 8 pieces
200g (7oz) sumac (available from Middle Eastern grocers)
grated rind of **4** oranges
6 green chillies, deseeded and chopped
100ml (3½fl oz) olive oil
1 large stone bass (also know as wreckfish), gutted, scaled and gills removed (your fishmonger will oblige)
1 tbsp toasted fennel seeds
salt and freshly ground black pepper

1   Cook the fennel in boiling, salted water until tender. Drain off the water and allow the fennel to cool.

2   To make the marinade, mix the sumac, orange rind and chopped green chillies with the olive oil and rub this mixture onto the skin and inside the fish. Set aside in the refrigerator for 10 minutes. Preheat the oven to 200°C/fan 180°C/400°F/gas mark 6.

3   Mix the blanched fennel with the toasted fennel seeds and stuff this mixture into the cavity of the fish.

4   Season with salt and pepper and roast in the oven for 25 minutes. Serve with salad and citrus segments.

Barbecue Pulled Pork
Tom Adams | Pitt Cue Co.

The key to this roast is to ensure the pork is soft and moist and that the fat dotted throughout is dark and caramelized. It might take a long time to cook, but once you taste the end result, you won't complain.

**MAKE ENOUGH FOR
16 SANDWICHES**

For the pork rub
10g (½oz) fennel seeds
1 tsp cumin seeds
1 tsp black peppercorns
1 tsp coriander seeds
100g (3½oz) dark brown sugar
50g (2oz) granulated sugar
10g (½oz) garlic powder
100g (3½oz) fine salt
15g (½oz) smoked paprika
30g (1oz) paprika
1 tsp dried oregano
1 tsp cayenne pepper

For the pork
1 pork neck end shoulder,
  weighing 4–5kg (8lb 14oz–11lb),
  skinned
200ml (⅓ pint) barbecue sauce
Maldon salt and freshly ground
  black pepper

For the pork rub

1 Toast the fennel seeds, cumin seeds, peppercorns and coriander seeds in a dry pan over a medium heat for a few minutes, shaking the pan until the spices release an aroma. Tip into a bowl and leave to cool.

2 Blitz the toasted spices in a blender to a rough powder. Combine with the remaining rub ingredients and mix thoroughly.

For the pork

1 Prepare a barbecue for smoking and set the temperature to 105°C (220°F). A shoulder of pork is pretty forgiving, but keeping a constant temperature will produce the best results. Once a decent bark starts to form, the smoke no longer effectively penetrates the meat so there is no point continuing to add more wood chunks after the first few hours of cooking.

2 Evenly massage the meat with 200g (7oz) of the rub, then smoke it on the barbecue, making sure it is fat (skin) side up. It can take up to 16 hours but can be ready any time after 14 hours, so keep an eye on it and have your meat probe to hand. Cooking times can vary massively – some pork just takes longer than others. The internal temperature should reach 88–90°C (190–194°F). Once it hits this temperature the butt will have a thick bark and be very dark. It will not be burnt, and will not taste burnt, so don't panic. The blade bone should pull out with little resistance and the shoulder should fall in on itself if pressed gently from above. At this stage remove the pork and set aside to rest, wrapped in foil, for 30 minutes.

3 Unwrap the pork and turn it upside down so the spinal bones are facing upwards. Carefully remove the spinal and rib bones from the underside of the shoulder. The small bones are very sharp, so be scrupulous. The meat around these bones is particularly special, so dig deep and work between the bones to find all you can. Remove the blade bone and the piece of tough cartilage that sits at the tip.

4 Start to work the meat and pull it apart. A correctly cooked shoulder should not take much work. An over-pulled shoulder will be mushy, so keep the meat in big chunks and strands. Add 50g (2oz) rub or to taste, sprinkling it evenly like seasoning. Add the barbecue sauce and work this all through the meat. Check for seasoning, adding pepper and sea salt to taste. Serve immediately, in warm rolls with pickles and slaw.

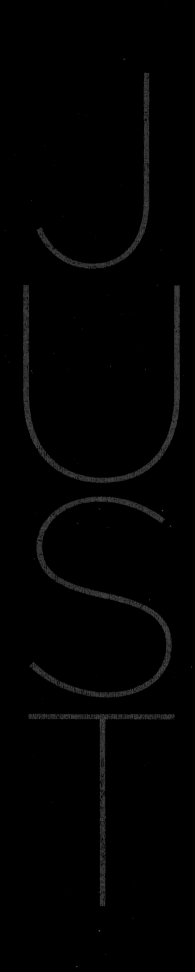

DESSERTS

Rhubarb and Custard Tart
Simon Schama

The classic combination of rhubarb and custard is given a sophisticated make over by Simon Schama. The really ingenious part, though, is the pastry recipe, that goes against all traditional beliefs, but works like a charm.

SERVES 8

For the filling
500g (1lb 2oz) rhubarb, cut into 3cm (1¼in) chunks
50g (1¾oz) caster sugar
1 tbsp lemon juice
30g (1oz) unsalted butter

For the custard
3 large eggs
200ml (⅓ pint) double cream or whole-milk yoghurt
1 tbsp vanilla extract
50g (1¾oz) caster sugar

For the pastry shell
90g (3¼oz) unsalted butter, diced, plus extra for greasing
3 tbsp water
1 tbsp vegetable oil such as safflower or canola
good pinch of salt
60g (2¼oz) caster sugar
170g (6oz) plain flour

Chef's Tip
Don't cook your rhubarb in an iron, aluminium or a copper pan as this will turn the fruit brown.

For the filling
1   Mix the rhubarb, sugar and lemon juice in a glass bowl and set aside for 15 minutes. Meanwhile, melt the butter in a medium-large saucepan. Add the rhubarb mixture and cook over a medium heat for about 5 minutes or until the rhubarb chunks are tender but still intact. Don't leave the kitchen! You don't want the rhubarb to disintegrate, which it does very quickly. When tender, remove from the heat and allow to cool.

For the custard
1   In a food processor, whizz the eggs, cream or yoghurt, vanilla extract and sugar to thicken and smooth the custard.

For the pastry shell
1   Preheat the oven to 210°C/fan 190°C/410°F/gas mark 6½. Grease a 22cm (8½in) loose-based tart tin.

2   Set the diced butter, water, oil, salt and sugar in an ovenproof bowl. Heat the mixture for around 20 minutes until it is bubbling and just beginning to brown.

3   Remove – remember those oven gloves – and quickly stir in the flour with a wooden spoon or spatula. It will – amazingly – cohere; work it into a ball that comes away from the sides of the bowl with the spatula. Set the pastry blob in the middle of the prepared tart tin and flatten a little.

4   When cool enough to handle – this will happen quicker than you think – press the pastry ball over the base of the tart tin, working with the heel of your hand from the centre towards the sides. More miracles – the pastry will stay fairly intact as you do this. Go for it, using your fingers to press the pastry up the grooved sides of the tart tin. Prick a few fork holes in the base of the shell. Set the pastry-lined tart tin in the oven and bake for about 15 minutes until golden, then reduce the oven temperature to 185°C/fan 165°C/360°F/gas mark 4.

5   Take the shell out of the oven and, using a rubber spatula, fill it with your rhubarb mix, then pour over the custard, leaving chunks of rhubarb poking above the surface of tart. Bake for around 40 minutes until the tart is golden – take care to ensure it doesn't brown. Cool the tart on a rack until you can safely and carefully remove it from the tin.

Strawberry and Pistachio Crumble
Marcus Eaves | L'Autre Pied

This original and eye-catching dessert might look complicated to make but, as Marcus Eaves explained to *GQ*, it really is a dish in which the individual components are straightforward to prepare and the rest is down to assembling them to look pretty.

SERVES 4

600g (1lb 5oz) strawberries, hulled and quartered
60g (2¼oz) caster sugar
100g (3½oz) butter
100g (3½oz) plain flour
50g (1¾oz) ground almonds
50g (1¾oz) pistachios, chopped
10 basil leaves, chopped
100g (3½oz) crème fraîche
30g (1oz) icing sugar

1   Mix the strawberries with the caster sugar and leave to macerate for 1 hour.

2   Preheat the oven to 180°C/fan 160°C/350°F/gas mark 4. To prepare the crumble mix, rub together the butter, flour, almonds and pistachios (reserve a few chopped pistachios for sprinkling) between your fingertips. Tip the mixture on to a baking tray and cook in the oven for about 20 minutes or until it is golden brown.

3   Whisk together the basil, crème fraîche and the icing sugar until thick.

4   Layer the crumble and the strawberries in Martini glasses. Add a generous serving of basil crème fraîche on top of each serving, then sprinkle over a few chopped pistachios.

Caramelized Apple Tart
Richard Davies | The Bybrook Restaurant

By using ready-made puff pastry, this tarte tatin by Richard Davies delivers maximum results from minimum effort. The rich caramel sauce and caramel powder compliment the crisp sharpness of the Granny Smiths perfectly, especially with a dollop of clotted cream on the side.

SERVES 4

For the sauce
100g (3½oz) caster sugar
140ml (4½fl oz) double cream

For the tart
100g (3½oz) caster sugar
250g (9oz) puff pastry
4 Granny Smith apples, peeled and cored
Cornish clotted cream ice cream, to serve
Icing sugar, to dust

For the sauce

1 Place the caster sugar in a clean saucepan set over a medium heat. Heat gently, stirring, until the sugar is golden brown, then remove the caramel from the heat and allow it to cool for 1 minute. Add the cream and bring to the boil, then reduce the heat and simmer until all the caramel has dissolved into the cream. Pass this mixture through a sieve and set aside.

For the tart

1 Put the caster sugar into a pan and cook until golden brown, as above. Carefully pour the caramel onto a sheet of baking paper and leave it to set. Once it is hard, put it in a food processor and pulse it to a sugar-like powder.

2 Preheat the oven to 190°C/fan 170°C/375°F/gas mark 5. Roll out the puff pastry to an even thickness of 3–4mm (⅛–¼in), then cut it into 10cm (4in) diameter discs and pop these in the freezer. Meanwhile, cut the apples in half vertically, then cut them into 2mm (1/16 in) slices horizontally across the apple halves.

3 Remove the tart cases from the freezer and fan out the apple slices around the cases, leaving a 3mm (⅛in) gap between the apples and the edges of the pastry. Dust with the caramel powder and bake for 20–30 minutes, or until the underside of the pastry is crisp. Serve with the caramel sauce, Cornish clotted cream ice cream and a light dusting of icing sugar.

Ice Cream Sandwich
with Salted Caramel Sauce
James Adams | Gail's Kitchen

Artisan bakery chain Gail's Kitchen specializes in all things bready, but they don't stop once their loaves are out of the oven. Using their delicious brioche as a base, head chef James Adams has created an ice cream sandwich with an irresistible sweet and salty caramel sauce.

SERVES 3

For the vanilla ice cream
400ml (14fl oz) milk
600ml (1 pint) double cream
9 egg yolks
175g (6oz) caster sugar
1 vanilla pod, split lengthways

For the salted caramel sauce
100ml (3½fl oz) water
400g (13oz) caster sugar
50g (2oz) golden syrup
100g (3½oz) salted butter, cubed
100ml (3½fl oz) double cream
100g (3½oz) crème fraîche

For the bread
100g (3½oz) ground cinnamon
100g (3½oz) caster sugar
2 slices brioche per person
butter, for frying

For the vanilla ice cream
1 Put the milk in a large pan with the cream, vanilla pod and half the sugar and heat over a low heat until steaming hot.

2 In a separate large bowl, blanche the yolks and the other half of the sugar.

3 Once the milk is steaming, pour it over the yolk mixture a third at a time, stirring after each addition. Then pour the mixture back into the pan over a medium heat and keep stirring. Heat to 80–83°C (176–181°F – use a sugar thermometer), then pour into a bowl set in a sink of iced water to cool. Once cool, discard the vanilla pod and pour the mixture into your ice cream machine and churn according to the manufacturer's instructions.

For the salted caramel sauce
1 Put the water, sugar and golden syrup in a heavy-based pan and heat – first over a low heat until the sugar has dissolved, then increase the temperature. When the mixture becomes very dark and smoking, take the pan off the heat and stir in the butter, cream and crème fraîche.

2 Put the pan back on the heat and bring the mixture to the boil, then remove from the heat and set aside.

For the bread
1 Mix the cinnamon and sugar together and sprinkle over both sides of the brioche slices. Melt a little butter in a large frying pan over a medium heat and fry the slices until golden on each side.

To serve
Sandwich a layer of the vanilla ice cream between two hot slices of brioche, then pour the salted caramel sauce over the top. Eat at once.

Crème Caramel
Richard Corrigan | Corrigan's Mayfair

Practically the official dessert of France, crème caramel is simple to make but easy to get wrong if you are careless, Richard Corrigan told *GQ*. And remember – this is a dish best served cold, as the low temperature brings out the best in the light custard.

SERVES 4

1 vanilla pod, split lengthways
1.2 litres (2 pints) milk
6 eggs
3 egg yolks
175g (6oz) caster sugar

For the caramel
140g (5oz) caster sugar
2 tbsp water

1 Preheat the oven to 180°C/fan 160°C/350°F/gas mark 4. First make the caramel. Put the sugar and water in a medium frying pan and bring to the boil. Cook for 4–5 minutes over a high heat without stirring, swirling the pan occasionally until the sugar has dissolved and turned a caramel colour. Divide the caramel between 4 x 150ml (5½ fl oz) ramekins making sure to coat the bottom of each ramekin.

2 Split the vanilla pod lengthways and remove the seeds. Place the seeds and the pod in a saucepan with the milk and warm over a low heat – do not let it boil.

3 Place the eggs and yolks in a bowl with the sugar and whisk until smooth. Gradually whisk in the warm milk a little at a time. Strain the mixture through a fine sieve, remove the vanilla pod, then pour into the ramekins.

4 Place the ramekins in a deep roasting tin and pour boiling water into the tin to come two-thirds up the side of the ramekins. Bake in the oven for 15–20 minutes or until the custards are just set. Remove from the oven and leave to cool. Refrigerate for 30–40 minutes before turning out to serve.

Chef's Tip
Use a heavy-based pan for making the caramel. Don't stir it, or crystals will form around the edges of the pan. To prevent this, use a damp pastry brush and run it around the edges of the pan.

Buttermilk Panna Cotta with Rhubarb
Bryn Williams | Odette's

Get the best from sweet early season rhubarb by poaching it with ginger wine. The pink veg should be just tender so that it still retains its shape, giving you a contrasting texture to the smooth panna cotta.

SERVES 4

3 gelatine leaves
250ml (9fl oz) double cream
100g (3½oz) caster sugar
1 fresh vanilla pod
250ml (9fl oz) cold buttermilk
200ml (⅓ pint) ginger wine
75g (2½oz) light soft brown sugar
1 strip of orange rind
250g (9oz) rhubarb cut into 2cm (¾in) batons

1 Soak the gelatine in cold water until soft. In a large pan, combine the double cream, 80g (3oz) of the caster sugar and the vanilla pod and bring to the boil. Remove the vanilla pod, add the softened gelatine to the hot liquid and stir until it has dissolved. Then pour the liquid onto the cold buttermilk and whisk together. Pour the mixture into 4 Martini glasses and place them in the refrigerator for 1–2 hours to set.

2 While the panna cotta is setting, gently heat the ginger wine with the soft brown sugar, remaining caster sugar and orange rind in a large shallow pan until the sugar has dissolved. Add the rhubarb and poach gently for 4–6 minutes or until soft. Leave the rhubarb to cool in the liquid.

3 When the panna cotta is set and the rhubarb is cold, divide the rhubarb into 4 portions. Put 1 of these onto each panna cotta. Pour some of the liquid from the rhubarb on top and serve immediately.

Chef's Tip
The panna cotta itself can be prepared the day before and left to set in the refrigerator overnight. This will save time on the day, when you can simply concentrate on preparing the rhubarb topping.

White Chocolate Mousse with Mixed Berry Compote Maria Balfour

A light and fruity end to any meal, Maria Balfour's creamy chocolate mousse, served with a sweet compote, is ideal any time but works best in summer when the berries are in season and are plentiful.

SERVES 6

For the mousse
500g (1lb 2oz) white chocolate, broken into pieces
600ml (1 pint) double cream

For the fruit compote
1 punnet blackberries
1 punnet blueberries
1 punnet raspberries
115g (4oz) caster sugar

fresh mint sprigs, to serve

For the mousse
1 Fill a saucepan with 10cm (4in) water and bring to a simmer. Place the chocolate in a heatproof bowl and put the bowl on top of the pan of simmering water, stirring occasionally, so that the chocolate melts.

2 Whip the double cream until it clings to the whisk but is still slightly floppy.

3 Fold the chocolate into the cream, ensuring there are no lumps. Pour this mixture into a bowl and leave it in the refrigerator to set.

For the fruit compote
1 Put the berries and sugar into a saucepan and simmer over a medium heat until the fruit has broken down and has released its juices. Pour the compote into a jug or bowl and set aside to cool.

2 Serve the mousse with the compote and finish with a mint sprig.

Beetroot Sorbet
Jason Atherton | Pollen Street Social

It might seem strange to use beetroot for a sorbet, but Jason Atherton's recipe using that most colourful of root vegetables manages to be sweet and earthy in equal measure. You will need to buy an ice cream machine (if you don't have one) to make the sorbet, but you'll be glad you did.

SERVES 4

For the purée
1.5kg (3lb 5oz) washed and chopped beetroot
50g (1¾oz) caster sugar
5 sprigs of thyme, leaves picked

For the sorbet
500g (1lb 2oz) beetroot purée (*see* above)
50g (1¾oz) glucose liquid
100ml (3½fl oz) stock syrup
lemon juice

For the beetroot reduction
1 large beetroot, cut into 1cm (½in) dice

For the jelly
500ml (18fl oz) beetroot reduction (*see* above)
250ml (9fl oz) stock syrup
4 bronze leaf gelatine leaves

For the beetroot discs
1 large beetroot
a little beetroot reduction
a little stock syrup

blackberries, halved, to decorate

Chef's Tip
As well as a dessert, this sorbet can be prepared as a savoury dish. Make an avocado purée and put it into a Martini glass, then cover with crab salad and pop the sorbet on top.

For the purée
Boil the beetroot with the sugar and thyme sprigs until cooked, then keep it immersed in just enough water to cover it for about 30 minutes. Return the pan to the heat and reduce the water until the beetroot is almost dry, but not quite. Remove the thyme, then blitz the beetroot in a blender and pass it through a fine sieve.

For the sorbet
Place all the ingredients for the sorbet (using the lemon juice to taste) into an ice cream machine, then freeze according to the manufacturer's instructions.

To make the beetroot reduction
Put the diced beetroot in a pan of water, bring to the boil and simmer until the beet is cooked. Blitz with an immersion blender to smash up and release the flavour. Pass the beetroot through a chinois, then return it to the pan and reduce to it to a syrup.

For the jelly
Mix the beetroot reduction with the stock syrup, then dissolve the gelatine in the mixture.

For the beetroot discs
Thinly slice the raw beetroot and cut into rounds with a biscuit cutter. Place these in a small sous-vide bag with a little beetroot reduction and a little syrup and cook in a water bath at 80°C (176°F) until cooked through. Serve alongside the sorbet, decorated with blackberries.

To serve
Serve the sorbet with the beetroot discs and some jelly, decorated with the halved blackberries.

Brownies
Allegra McEvedy | Leon

Instead of the classic white flour, sugar and butter-loaded varieties, Allegra McEvedy keeps her brownies wheat-free and uses espresso, toasted almonds and good chocolate to make them rich and indulgent. One, you will discover, is simply not enough...

MAKES 12

180g (6oz) unsalted butter, plus extra for greasing
200g (7oz) dark chocolate (Belgian, 54 per cent cocoa solids)
2 tsp espresso or other very strong coffee, at room temperature
1 tsp organic cold-pressed sweet orange oil or the finely grated rind of 1 orange
4 free-range eggs
80g (3oz) sweet Spanish almonds (skin on), toasted and chopped
100g (3½oz) ground sweet Spanish almonds
160g (5¾oz) dark chocolate chunks (Belgian, 54 per cent cocoa solids)
160g (5¾oz) very-dark chocolate chunks (Belgian, 72 per cent cocoa solids)
150g (5½oz) fructose
a pinch of sea salt
3–4 drops Madagascan bourbon vanilla extract

1 Preheat the oven to 180°C/fan 160°C/350°F/ gas mark 4. Melt the butter in a pan and, at the same time, melt the dark chocolate in a heatproof bowl set over a pan of hot water. Stir the chocolate well, ensure it's fully melted and be careful not to burn it.

2 Once the butter is melted and cooled slightly, add the coffee and melted chocolate and stir well, then add whichever orange bits you're using.

3 When making the batter mix, avoid adding anything too hot or too cold to the mix, as it may shrink, so have all your ingredients at room temperature – don't use them straight from the refrigerator. To ensure a nice, even brownie mix, take special care to place the ingredients into the mixing bowl in the following order. Put the eggs in first, then all the almonds, then the dark chocolate chunks and very dark chocolate chunks and, lastly, the fructose. Stir in the salt and vanilla, followed by the butter, and the coffee and orange mixture. Mix well until creamy and thickened. Don't overmix – too much air will cause the brownie to crumble when baked.

4 Spoon the mixture into a well-buttered 30 x 30cm (12 x 12in) baking pan and bake for 20–25 minutes. Take care not to overbake. The brownie is ready when the edges are slightly crusty and the middle is still soft. Bear in mind that fructose goes much darker than sugar when baked and the brownie will have a glossy sheen – it may not look baked even when it is. Allow to cool in the pan before cutting into brownies.

Organic Coffee Ice Cream
Virgilio Martinez | Lima

There is more to Peruvian cuisine than the pisco sour, as new and critically-acclaimed restaurants such as Lima are demonstrating. Chef Virgilio Martinez has brought his modern interpretation of some of Peru's most authentic dishes to the capital, and this dessert showcases his talents beautifully.

MAKES 10 SCOOPS

For the ice cream
250ml (9fl oz) whole milk
200g (7oz) caster sugar
a pinch of salt
100g (3½oz) whole organic coffee beans, crushed
200ml (⅓ pint) double cream
5 egg yolks
60g (2¼oz) organic ground coffee

For the maca root syrup
400g (14oz) grated chancaca (a raw, unrefined Latin American cane sugar with a high molasses content)
200ml (⅓ pint) water
1 tbsp maca root powder

For the coconut crumbs
100g (3½oz) chancaca, grated
200g (7oz) desiccated coconut

edible flowers (such as pansies), to decorate

1 First make the ice cream. Bring the milk, sugar, salt and the crushed coffee beans to the boil for 2 minutes, then simmer for a further 5 minutes and set aside.

2 At the same time, warm the cream (but not to higher than 63°C/145°F – use a thermometer), then add the egg yolks and whisk to form a custard. Add the ground coffee and whisk again to form a smooth mix.

3 Place the coffee-infused milk back on the heat and simmer for 2 minutes, then pass it through a fine sieve (discard the beans). While it is still warm (do not boil it), add the cream mix and whisk. Place the mixture in the refrigerator, then freeze in an ice cream machine according to the manufacturer's instructions.

4 To make the maca root syrup, dissolve the grated chancaca in the water to form a syrup. Mix in the maca root powder, then pass the mixture through a fine sieve if necessary.

5 Mix the chancaca with the desiccated coconut to make the coconut crumbs.

6 To serve, drizzle the maca root syrup on each plate, sprinkle the coconut crumbs in the centre, then add a scoop of organic coffee ice cream on top. Serve immediately decorated with edible flowers.

Spice Cakes with Walnuts and Figs

Richard Corrigan | Bentley's Oyster Bar & Grill

You don't need to decorate this dessert with a sprig of holly to know that it is a perfect way to end a festive Christmas feast. Richard Corrigan relies on plenty of ground spices to give this cake a fragrant and unforgettable flavour.

SERVES 6

250g (9oz) butter, plus extra for greasing
50g (1¾oz) honey
100g (3½oz) flour
300g (10½oz) granulated sugar
50g (1¾oz) ground almonds
½ tbsp baking powder
1 tsp ground cinnamon
½ tsp ground ginger
1 tsp mixed spice
1 tsp liquorice powder
1 tsp Chinese five spice
8–9 egg whites, whisked to soft peaks

To serve
6 ripe figs
walnuts, shelled
vanilla ice cream

1   Preheat the oven to 200°C/fan 180°C/400°F/gas mark 6. Melt the butter in a saucepan and, when it is golden brown, add the honey. Take the mixture off the heat and allow it to cool.

2   Mix all the dry ingredients together, then stir in the melted butter and beaten egg whites.

3   Grease 6 ramekins (or a muffin tin) with butter and fill with the cake mix. Bake for 10–12 minutes. Serve with ripe figs, shelled walnuts and a scoop of vanilla ice cream.

Chef's Tip
Make sure you use nice ripe figs, preferably black mission figs. You could toast the walnuts gently to give an added depth of flavour.

COCKTAIL